KT-486-982

Mexico

by Fiona Dunlop

Fiona Dunlop has indulged her parallel tastes
for the tropics and for developing countries
by writing AA Explorer guides on Singapore
& Malaysia, Indonesia, Vietnam, Costa Rica,
Mexico, and India. During a 15-year sojourn
in Paris she wrote *Explorer Paris* as well
as working in and covering the arts scene
for numerous publications. She is now based
in London.

Above: *the much-loved traditional* mariachi *band is found
all over Mexico*

AA Publishing

Above: image of the Virgin of Guadalupe, Mexico City

Written by Fiona Dunlop
Updated by Larry Dunmire

First published 1999
Reprinted Aug 2000
Reprinted 2001. Information verified and updated.
Reprinted Oct 2002. Reprinted Jan 2004, May 2004
This edition 2005. Information verified and updated.

Published by AA Publishing, a trading name of Automobile Association Developments Limited, whose registered office is Southwood East, Apollo Rise, Farnborough, Hampshire, GU14 0JW. Registered number 1878835.

Find out more about AA Publishing and the wide range of travel publications and services the AA provides by visiting our website at www.theAA.com/bookshop

A01990

Colour separation: Keenes, Andover, Hampshire
Printed and bound in Italy by Printer Trento S.r.l.

Contents

About this Book

KEY TO SYMBOLS

✚ map reference to the maps found in the What to See section

✉ address or location

☎ telephone number

🕐 opening times

🍴 restaurant or café on premises or nearby

Ⓜ nearest subway train station

🚌 nearest bus/tram route

🚊 nearest train station

⛴ ferry crossings and boat excursions

✈ travel by air

ℹ tourist information

♿ facilities for visitors with disabilities

✋ admission charge

↔ other places of interest nearby

❓ other practical information

➤ indicates the page where you will find a fuller description

---

This book is divided into five sections to cover the most important aspects of your visit to Mexico.

Viewing Mexico pages 5–14
An introduction to Mexico by the author.
  Mexico's Features
  Essence of Mexico
  The Shaping of Mexico
  Peace and Quiet
  Mexico's Famous

Top Ten pages 15–26
The author's choice of the Top Ten places to see in Mexico, listed in alphabetical order, each with practical information.

What to See pages 27–90
The five main areas of Mexico, each with its own brief introduction and an alphabetical listing of the main attractions.
  Practical information
  Snippets of 'Did you know…' information
  3 suggested walks
  4 suggested tours
  2 features

Where To… pages 91–116
Detailed listings of the best places to eat, stay, shop, take the children, and be entertained.

Practical Matters pages 117–24
A highly visual section containing essential travel information.

Maps
All map references are to the individual maps found in the What to See section of this guide.
For example, Palenque has the reference ✚ 73E1 – indicating the page on which the map is located and the grid square in which the archaeological site is to be found. A list of the maps that have been used in this travel guide can be found in the index.

Prices
Where appropriate, an indication of the cost of an establishment is given by **$** signs:

$$$ denotes higher prices,
$$ denotes average prices, while
$ denotes lower charges.

Star Ratings
Most of the places described in this book have been given a separate rating:
✪✪✪   Do not miss
✪✪   Highly recommended
✪   Worth seeing

Viewing
Mexico

Above: *a cactus blooms in the Baja California desert*
Right: *a pilgrim advances towards the Basílica de Guadalupe*

Fiona Dunlop's Mexico

NAFTA

In 1994 Mexico, the U.S.A. and Canada inaugurated the North American Free Trade Agreement (NAFTA). This momentous economic union is designed to gradually break down all trade barriers between the three countries over a 15-year period, and has already produced an influx of American capital, particularly in the Cancún area, and in new services in the northern cities. Mexico is certainly benefiting from it economically, with 80 percent of its exports heading north, but it is questionable how positive the long-term cultural effects will be.

Shoeshiners are part of the zócalo *picture in every Mexican town*

Traveling through Mexico is a strangely familiar experience, not just because I've been there before, but because so much of it has clear European and North American influences. But behind this hybrid facade lies the more secret life of the indigenous people, whose ancestors erected the most incredible pyramids and structures, observed and worshipped the stars, and were playing around with the concept of zero some 1,500 years ago while Europe was still lost in the Dark Ages.

Traditional crafts reflect the imagination and flair of the Mexicans, whether intricate handweavings, touchingly crude Tarahumara animal carvings, exquisite ceramics and silverware, or tin *milagros* (votive offerings to saints). Indigenous men and women cling to their traditional dress, with endless extraordinary regional variations. But far from being a picture of a tranquil, time-honored existence, these people continue to suffer at the hands of landowners and political interests, a fact that visitors will become aware of.

Then there is Mexico's magnificent Spanish heritage, one of dazzling baroque masterpieces and grid-like urban layouts. The inevitable *zócalo*, the social crossroads of every town, is the shoeshiners' workplace and for me, the smell of shoe-polish can only mean Mexico. In contrast, as the northern border draws closer, there is a distinct feel of growing prosperity and increasing Americanization. But this doesn't mean that *ahorita* means anything other than "in a short while." Long may it continue!

Mexico's Features

Geography

- Mexico's total area is 1,958,201sq km (755,866sq miles), about a quarter of the size of the U.S.A.
- The highest peak is the Pico de Orizaba (5,700m).
- Mexico City lies at an altitude of 2,240m.
- Mexico's coastline totals 10,150km (6,307 miles).
- Mexico is home to nearly 30,000 species of flowering plants, 1,000 species of birds, 2,000 of fish and about 450 of mammals.

Socio-economic

- Mexico is the world's most populous Spanish-speaking country.
- The population is approximately 100 million, with between 20 and 30 million inhabiting the capital.
- The indigenous population is estimated to be nearly 30 million.
- 56 indigenous languages survive.
- 89.7 percent of Mexicans are Catholics.
- An estimated 45 million Mexicans live in conditions of extreme poverty.
- 1.6 million Mexicans were arrested in 2000 while attempting to cross illegally into the U.S.A.
- 70 years of PRI (Partido Revoluionario Institucional) rule was ended in 2000 when Mexicans voted overwhelmingly for the National Action Party (NAP).

Various

- There are 200 or so varieties of chilli.
- 87 percent of Mexico's tequila exports go to the U.S.A.
- *Pulque*, a pre-Hispanic beer brewed from the maguey plant, still represents about 10 percent of Mexico's total alcohol consumption.

Indigenous People
The majority of Mexicans are *mestizos*, mixed Spanish and Mexican blood, with pure indigenous groups concentrated mainly in the south, in Oaxaca, Chiapas, and the Yucatán peninsula. Other pockets are found in Michoacán (Tarascans), in the mountains of Nayarit and Tabasco (Huichols) and in the rugged northern canyons (Tarahumara).

The source of pulque, mezcal, *and tequila: the blue maguey or agave plant*

Essence of Mexico

Above: *a Toltec warrior at Tula*
Right: *detail of Quetzalcóatl, the plumed serpent god*

Below: *strumming mariachis in their home town of Guadalajara*

Few nations can rival Mexico's turbulent history, and few can claim such a cultural diversity. From the enigmatic giant heads of the Olmecs and the baroque outpourings of the Spaniards, to the

stark clean lines of contemporary architecture and time-honored skills of craftspeople, Mexico proudly displays a richly creative pulse. Reflecting this are the contrasts of the land itself —tropical rainforests in Chiapas, desert in Baja California, volcanoes and lakes in the center and *cenotes* (sinkholes) in the Yucatán. It is a country that excites, stimulates, and awes. Surprises lurk around every corner.

THE **10** ESSENTIALS

If you only have a short time to visit Mexico, or would like to get a really complete picture of the country, here are the essentials:

- **Steep yourself** in colonial history in Mexico City's Centro Histórico, paying homage to the last remnants of the proud Aztec culture at the Templo Mayor (➤ 39), before retreating to a restaurant to sample pre-Hispanic cuisine.
- **Indulge in countless varieties** of tequila at the Plaza Garibaldi in Mexico City, while being serenaded by *mariachi* sounds. Do the same thing in Guadalajara (➤ 43), where the *mariachis* have their origins, or in Veracruz (➤ 81), where the *marimba* joins the band.
- **Stretch out on a Pacific beach** under a shady *palapa* at Huatulco, Puerto Vallarta, or Puerto Escondido, or swim with pelicans and whales in Baja California.
- **Visit an indigenous village** in Chiapas, such as San Juan Chamula (➤ 79), to see a unique synthesis of ancient Maya worship and Catholic rituals.
- **Admire the prowess** of a baroque masterpiece and the fertile imagination of its sculptors in Taxco, Puebla, Cuernavaca, Querétaro, or Oaxaca.
- **Explore the markets** of towns such as Pátzcuaro (➤ 45) or Oaxaca (➤ 72), where the craft work is outstanding, then tour the surrounding villages to observe craftspeople at work.
- **Take a boat tour** on a lagoon to observe Mexico's rich bird life, both native and migratory, at San Blas (➤ 67).
- **Get a close-up** of one of Mexico's seismic giants: Popocatépetl, neighboring Iztaccíhuatl, Pico de Orizaba, or the Cofre de Perote, near Jalapa.
- **Explore a less-visited** archaeological site such as Yagul (➤ 76) to soak up pre-Hispanic history without the crowds.
- **Go scuba diving or snorkeling** at Cozumel (➤ 87) or Isla Mujeres (➤ 88) in the company of technicolored tropical fish.

Products of the land range from a shot of tequila to a tantalizing choice of tropical fruits

The Shaping of Mexico

60000–8000 BC
Waves of nomadic hunters cross the Bering Strait from Mongolia and gradually move south.

c1200 BC–AD 100
Development of the Olmec culture along the Gulf of Mexico is followed by the Zapotecs at Monte Albán, the rise of El Tajín and, at the beginning of the Christian era, of Teotihuacán.

600–900
Zenith of Mayan culture stretching from the Yucatán peninsula to Guatemala. End of the Classic period between the 9th and 10th centuries; rise of the Toltecs at Tula and Mixtecs in Oaxaca.

1400s
Aztecs dominate the heart of Mexico.

1502–20
Rule of Moctezuma II from the Aztec capital, Tenochtitlán (today's Mexico City).

1519
Hernán Cortés lands near Veracruz and marches on the Aztec capital.

The Spanish invaders lusted for gold

1521
The Aztec capital finally falls and Moctezuma's successor, Cuauhtémoc, is captured and killed three years later.

1535
Spanish vice-regal system is set up. Spread of the *encomienda* system (vast tracts of land given to conquerors) and virtual Indian slavery.

1767–1804
Expulsion of the Jesuits: the remaining Catholic Church is Mexico's greatest landowner. Expropriation of all Church property in 1804 leads to chaos.

1810–20
Miguel Hidalgo calls for independence, sparking off a popular revolt. Mexico City falls to the insurgents in 1820.

1821
Mexico is granted independence from Spain under a constitutional monarchy. General Iturbide declares himself Emperor, but power passes to General Santa Ana, heading a new federal republic.

1836
The cattle ranchers of Texas, enraged by the abolition of slavery, rebel and declare their independence.

1845
Texas is annexed by the United States.

1846–48
The Mexican–American War ends with a treaty that loses Mexico half its former territory.

1857
Benito Juárez instigates reforms, plunging Mexico into a civil war that he wins in 1861. Inability to repay foreign debts leads to a joint attack by Spain, Britain, and France on Veracruz.

1864–67
Habsburg Archduke Maximilian rules as the puppet emperor of Mexico. Juárez obtains American backing; the French withdraw.

1876–1910
Dictatorship of Porfirio Díaz rebuilds the nation at the cost of civil liberties.

1911–17
Díaz is ousted in elections by the liberal Francisco Madero, backed by revolutionary groups of Zapata and Pancho Villa. Conflicting ideals lead to civil war, with Obregón and Carranza joining attempts to dislodge the new, American-backed President Huerta. The revolution officially ends in 1917 with a new

President Lázaro Cárdenas

constitution, but conflicts continue into the 1920s.

1934–40
President Lázaro Cárdenas introduces prosperity and civil peace by redistribution of land to peasants, nationalizations and generally boosting the Mexican national identity.

1946
The ruling party since 1929 is renamed Partido Revolucionario Institucional (PRI). Corruption increases.

1988–94
The presidency of Carlos Salinas de Gortari reveals untold corruption, political assassinations, violations of human rights, money-laundering, and an increasing chasm between rich and poor.

1994
As Mexico officially enters NAFTA (North American Free Trade Agreement), a band of insurgents ("Zapatistas") takes over parts of Chiapas, demanding indigenous rights.

1995
Devaluation of the *peso* by President Ernesto Zedillo heralds Mexico's deepest recession since the 1930s.

2000
Seventy years of PRI rule ends when the National Action Party wins the general election.

2004
Earthquake near Colima state kills 28, leaves 10,000 homeless.

Peace & Quiet

Mexico's diverse topography, roughly categorized into three altitudes, offers a bewildering choice of escapes for those in search of a return to nature. Hand-in-hand with the rainforest, sierras, scrub, pine forests, desert, and volcanic craters goes an equally varied wildlife, from iguanas, harpy eagles and quetzals to jaguars, Jesus Christ lizards, and grey whales.

Savannah, Sea and Cenotes

Visitors to the Yucatán peninsula should explore the Sian Ka'an Biosphere Reserve to see the savannah edging mangrove swamps and, on the horizon, the world's second-longest ocean reef. Pumas, white-tail deer, crocodiles, howler monkeys and some 300 bird species are all resident, best observed on a trek organized through Amigos de Sian Ka'an, in Cancún. On the north and west coast respectively, Río Lagartos and Celestún reserves are favorite nesting grounds for pink flamingos, and the tiny island of Isla Contoy remains a rewarding bird sanctuary. Elsewhere in this limestone plateau, dive, swim, or snorkel in one of the many *cenotes* (sinkholes).

Below: Mexico's rich wildlife includes the hyacinth macaw
Bottom: the Mexican deer

Jungle Wilds

Only about one-fifth of Mexico's original rainforest remains, mostly concentrated in Chiapas, where high rainfall helps maintain steamy jungles, much appreciated by macaws, toucans, parakeets, spider monkeys, and butterflies, and mammals such as jaguars and ocelots. Montes Azules is the most accessible ecotourism destination in this region, with trips arranged from Palenque or Tenosique deep into the Lacandon Forest. Mexico's largest cloud forest is at El Triunfo Biosphere Reserve, near Tapachula in the Sierra Madre range.

Coast to Hills

Beyond the Isthmus, in the state of Oaxaca, the land becomes noticeably drier. Nature-lovers should enjoy the diving facilities at Puerto Escondido and Huatulco. Here, too, are coastal wetlands such as the Lagunas de Chacahua and the turtle sanctuary of Mazunte. In stark contrast, the area around Catemaco (southeast of Veracruz) is dubbed "little Switzerland," while in the tiny state of Tabasco there are more coastal lagoons as well as savannah and jungle.

Volcano Territory

Central Mexico is the land of the volcanoes. The national park surrounding the twin peaks of Popocatépetl and Iztaccíhuatl, the crater lakes of Nevado de Toluca, and the more strenuous ascent of Pico de Orizaba all offer extensive hiking and climbing. The Michoacán village engulfed by the seismic activity of Paricutín in the 1940s offers a striking spectacle and can be explored on a horseback tour from Uruapan. Try also the Xochimilco Ecological Park (► 26) on the outskirts of Mexico City.

Desert

Endless scrub, sierra and desert characterize most of northern Mexico, with notable exceptions provided by the spectacular canyons of the Sierra Tarahumara and the coastal lagoons between Mazatlán and San Blas. The biosphere reserves of the islands in the Mar de Cortés have a spectacular 570 species of plants and the sea itself over 15 species of whales and porpoises. In Baja California, the Sierra de la Gigánta and the Desierto de Vizcaíno are home to puma and lynx, as well as exceptional desert landscapes and flora.

Ecotourism
Amigos de Sian Ka'an
Cancún ☎ (998) 884 9583

Associacion Mexicana de Tourismo de Aventura y Ecotourismo (AMTAVE)
☎ (998) 884 9780, fax: (998) 887 5469 (► 55)

Below: *a splash of white flowers on the Casahuata tree*
Bottom: *the dramatic volcanic lake of the Nevado de Toluca*

Mexico's Famous

Frida Kahlo

The darling of international feminist artists and collectors is Frida Kahlo (1907–54), the woman who battled with childhood polio, a near fatal tramway accident in her teens, and a lifetime of physical and psychological suffering to become one of Mexico's foremost 20th-century painters. Her bold images of flowers, birds, and animals gradually gave way to a tortuous series of agonising self-portraits, partly stimulated by her relationship with Diego Rivera (► below). Always extravagantly and eccentrically attired, Kahlo attended her last exhibition in Mexico City in her richest Zapotec costumes and jewelry, lying on a four-poster bed.

Enduring icons of Mexican art: Diego Rivera and Frida Kahlo

Moctezuma II
Moctezuma II, greatest of all Aztec emperors, was another of Mexico's tragic heroes. More given to meditation and learning than to warfare, he erroneously opened the doors of his palace to the Conquistadores. Convinced that Hernán Cortés was in reality the great god Quetzalcóatl returning from the east, Moctezuma showered him with priceless presents. However, even his semi-divine status among his people could not prevent him from being kidnapped by the Spaniards, or being killed.

Diego Rivera

Variously described as an ogre, a seducer, and a frog, Diego Rivera (1886–1957) is without doubt one of Mexico's greatest artistic geniuses. After indulging to the full in a decade of Bohemian life in Paris, Rivera returned to Mexico City in 1921 and began pioneering Mexican muralism, together with Orozco and Siqueiros. Much inspired by the Russian revolution, Rivera's stylized murals of class struggles, socialist ideals, and the violence perpetuated against Mexico's Indians plastered government buildings all over the country. His functionalist studio in San Angel and the Museo Anáhuacalli reveal his diverse interests, but above all his passion for pre-Hispanic cultures.

Emiliano Zapata

Emiliano Zapata (1879–1919), the most charismatic figure of the Mexican Revolution, was sadly destined for a treacherous end when he was ambushed and assassinated by order of President Carranza, a former ally. Zapata's rise to revolutionary power started in 1910 when he mobilized a band of peasant insurgents in the state of Morelos with his cry "Tierra y libertad!" ("land and freedom") and proceeded to redistribute millions of hectares of land. From his headquarters in Tlaltizapan (now a museum), Zapata led his *bandoleros* (peasant revolutionaries) into endless battles, and by 1912 controlled strategic points on the outskirts of the capital. In 1994 Zapata's name was revived by guerrilla leader Sub-Comandante Marcos to inspire a new revolt in Chiapas.

Top Ten

Above: *Palenque's towering Templo de las Inscripciones, home to King Pakal's tomb*
Right: *a fertility goddess from Veracruz at the Museo Nacional de Antropología*

15

1
Barranca del Cobre
(Copper Canyon)

 28B3

Daily 1st and 2nd class
train leaves Los Mochis
at 6AM, Chihuahua at
7AM

Airports at Los Mochis
and Chihuahua

Libertad 1300, 1st Floor,
Edificio Agustín Melgar,
Chihuahua

Chihuahua (► 54)

Easter processions
and dances peak on
Easter Fri

*Rugged canyons, spectacular waterfalls, old mining
villages, Jesuit missions, and the Chihuahua–
Pacifico railroad are the highlights here.*

Five times wider and one-and-a-half times deeper than the
Grand Canyon, the 35,000sq km (13,510sq miles) Barranca
del Cobre is rapidly becoming a major ecotourism destination. It is composed of five adjoining canyons sliced out
of the Sierra Madre Occidental, their sculpted ravines
offering startling extremes in climate and vegetation. In
winter the upper plateau may be blanketed in snow, while
on the canyon floors warm, balmy temperatures prevail; in
summer the Sierra Tarahumara is refreshingly cooler than
oven-like Chihuahua, though rain is abundant.

The most striking access to this region is by rail,
through 88 tunnels and over 39 bridges from Los Mochis,
near the Mar de Cortés, to Divisadero and Creel, or arriving
in the other less scenic direction from Chihuahua. The
main town is Creel. Facilities here include day trips on
horseback or by van into the surrounding canyons, to Lago
Arareco, Cascada de Cusararé, the hot springs of
Recohuata or the six-hour ride to Batopilas, a former silver-
mining town 2,000m (6,561ft) below on the canyon floor.
In the far north are the thundering waters of the Cascada
de Basaseáchic, a 246m (807ft) waterfall whose
spectacular pine-clad surroundings are now a national park.

The original inhabitants of this region, the Tarahumara,
now only number about 50,000. Their geographical
isolation has preserved their distinctive traditions that
climax during colorful Easter processions.

*A rare flat stretch on the
otherwise tortuous
Chihuahua–Pacifico
railroad*

2
Chichén Itzá

This archaeological site is the most popular in the Yucatán peninsula. Two distinct excavated zones present extraordinary and unique structures.

Jaguar heads have surveyed Chichén Itzá for over 1,400 years

Founded in AD 514 by a priest, this ceremonial centre experienced two peaks, from 600 to 900, and again from the late 10th century until 1196. Civil wars and cultural stagnation followed before Chichén and other northern Maya civilizations finally collapsed in 1441. When the Spaniards arrived a century later, they named the partially ruined structures according to mere supposition.

At the centre of the vast plaza in the northern group rises the striking Pyramid of Kukulkán. Its 365 steps and 52 base panels represent the solar year, and twice a year, at the spring and summer equinoxes, the shadows of the north staircase create a serpentine shape that joins the carved snakes' heads at the bottom. To the northwest is a ball court, the largest yet discovered in Mexico, lined with bas-reliefs of players. Overshadowing this is the Templo de los Jaguares (Temple of Jaguars), with extensive jaguar and eagle carvings. Beside it stands the macabre Tzompantli (Platform of Skulls), that once displayed the heads of sacrificial victims.

Across the plaza is the richly decorated Templo de los Guerreros (Warriors' Temple) with, at its base, an extensive, roofless colonnade, the Mil Columnas (Thousand Columns). From the platform high above, the entire plaza is surveyed by a much-photographed *chacmool* (seated human figure).

The highlight of the older group is the Caracol (snail), an elevated circular building once used for astronomical observations. Facing it is the ornately decorated Edificio de las Monjas (nunnery) and, between them, the Iglesia (church), crowned by a remarkable roof comb and adorned with masks of the rain god, Chac.

29F2

(985) 851 0097

Site and museum: daily 8–5; services: 8AM–10PM

Cafeteria ($)

ADO bus from Mérida, Calle 50

Tourist information offices in Mérida and Cancún

Expensive; free Sun

Sound and light show nightly: 8 in Spanish; 9 in English. Spring and autumn equinox celebrations

3
Guanajuato

✚ 42A2

✈ Flights from Mexico City

ℹ Plaza de la Paz 14
☎ (473) 732 1574

Alhóndiga de Granaditas

✉ Calle 28 de Septiembre

☎ (473) 732 1112

🕐 Tue–Sat 10–2, 4–6, Sun 10–3. Closed 25 Dec, 1 Jan, Easter Sun

A bird's-eye view of Guanajuato

Tumbling down a hillside in central Mexico is this gem of a town. Former silver wealth has left a legacy of superb colonial architecture.

Historically one of Mexico's most important towns, Guanajuato originally earned its status from its rich silver mines, founded in 1546. It never looked back and in 1989 was declared a world heritage site by UNESCO. A network of underground tunnels keeps traffic out of its central plazas and alleys, making it a joy to wander in, though less so to drive in as orientation is not easy.

On a hilltop overlooking the town are the old mines of La Valenciana (one still functions), next to a 1770s church containing three fine baroque altarpieces. Further along the Carretera Panorámica is the Museo de las Momías, another of Guanajuato's unique sights, containing over 100

mummified bodies retrieved from the local cemetery where they had been impeccably preserved in the mineral-rich soil.

In the town centre, the main attraction is the **Alhóndiga de Granaditas**, which houses the regional museum. This imposing building, originally a corn exchange, played a major role in the War of Independence when it became a fortress and later the macabre showcase for the heads of captured rebels. It now exhibits pre-Hispanic objects, altarpieces, religious paintings, and items related to the Independence struggle. A short walk east of here brings you to the grandiose University, one of the most important in Mexico and, just beyond, is the Templo de la Compañia de Jesús, a 1750s church with a remarkable facade. Immediately below is the focal point of town, the lively Jardín de la Unión, backed by the highly decorative Teatro Juárez.

4
Huatulco

Situated on what was once a deserted coastline, this fledgling resort offers dramatic scenery and excellent services.

Although Huatulco's string of nine bays were spotted by the Spanish conquistadores, they were never exploited as a port. For centuries, this idyllic fishing village slumbered peacefully before being earmarked in the early 1980s by Mexico's resort planners as a follow-up to Cancún. Progress was not always smooth; development suffered from the 1994–45 financial crisis and Hurricane Pauline in 1997. However, unlike other Pacific resorts, planners have learned from the mistakes elsewhere and produced an environmentally sensitive resort with low-rise hotels.

Today, Huatulco boasts an international airport, over 20 hotels, a marina, an 18-hole golf course and three developed beaches at Tangolunda (the most exclusive), Santa Cruz, and Chahue, as well as a lively inland village, La Crucecita, with budget accommodation. Other beaches remain blissfully untouched with, at the most, a few *palapa* restaurants. Between the pockets of hotels are jungle-clad hills and cliffs that are rich in wildlife. Activities include jungle motorbike expeditions, kayaking, snorkeling, and diving around the reefs in Huatulco's clear waters.

Although historical sights are totally absent, Huatulco boasts a modern *zócalo* at the center of La Crucecita. This animated hub is overlooked by a church, **Iglesia de Guadalupe**, worth visiting for its vast contemporary mural of the Virgen de Guadalupe that decorates the entire ceiling vault.

➕ 73D1

✈ Flights from Oaxaca, Mexico City

ℹ Boulevard Santa Cruz, corner Monte Albán, Bahía de Santa Cruz
☎ (958) 581 0176/0177

♿ Good

✋ Free

Iglesia de Guadalupe

✉ Calle Gardenia, La Crucecita

🕓 Daily 9–8

🍴 Cafés and restaurants ($–$$) on plaza

Bahía Tangolunda in Huatulco, backed by the moody Sierra Madre del Sur

5

Monte Albán
(White Mountain)

Clear, high-altitude light adds to the magic of Monte Albán

"White Mountain" sits atop a leveled hill above the valley of Oaxaca. Magnificent in scale, layout and setting, it is an absolute must–see.

+ 72C1

✉ 6km (4 miles) west of Oaxaca

☎ (951) 516 1215

🕐 Mon–Fri 8–5, Sat–Sun 9–3

🍴 Café ($) on site

🚌 Buses from Oaxaca, Calle Mina 518, every 30 minutes 8:30–3:30

✈ Numerous internal flights to Oaxaca

ℹ Sedetur: Independencia, corner García Vigil, Oaxaca ☎ (951) 516 0123

♿ Good to museum

✋ Moderate; free Sun

↔ Oaxaca (▶ 72)

Incredible 360-degree views of the barren hills surrounding Monte Albán give a strong sense of proximity to the gods, a fact recognized by the later Mixtecs, who used the abandoned site for offerings and burials between 1350 and the arrival of the Spaniards. The ancient Zapotec site was founded *c*500 BC and peaked between AD 500 and 600 with an estimated population of over 20,000. Like many other Mesoamerican sites, it was abandoned in the 8th century and, apart from its Mixtec interlude, fell into ruin.

From the site entrance and well-designed museum, a path winds uphill to the corner of the northern pyramid, where the breathtaking Gran Plaza opens up before you. To the left is a ball court, a palace, and small temple platforms, and opposite are three large temple structures. Between them a 300m plaza unfolds to the majestic steps of the southern pyramid. Other buildings are aligned down the center, yet the overall sense of space remains absolute from any vantage point.

Behind the northern pyramid are five tombs, the most elaborate being Tomb 104. East of this, near the access path, is Tomb 7, source of the fabulous Mixtec treasures displayed in Oaxaca's museum. On the western flank of the plaza, the Palacio de los Danzantes (Palace of the Dancers) was named after a series of stone slabs carved with dancing figures that stand around its base. There are countless theories about these oddly deformed figures.

6

Museo Nacional de Antropología

This museum is a must for any visitor to Mexico City, as it houses an exemplary display of the nation's indigenous cultures.

Built in the early 1960s, the Anthropological Museum does full justice to the complexities of Mexico's early civilizations through a dynamic display grouped according to regions. The focal point is a large semi-roofed courtyard fountain; surrounding it are the ground-floor galleries devoted to Mesoamerican artifacts and the upper floor to the rich diversity of surviving traditions among Mexico's indigenous populations. Another attraction is the museum's verdant location in Chapultepec Park, offering a leafy post-museum walk and plenty of local animation.

The ground-floor galleries start in the right-hand wing and follow an anti-clockwise direction around the courtyard. An introduction to world anthropology and ethnology continues with the origins of Mesoamerican man, before moving into what is termed pre-Classic civilisations (1700–200 BC). Then follow rooms dedicated to Teotihuacán, Tula (the militaristic Toltecs), México (the Aztecs), Oaxaca (Mixtecs and Zapotecs), the Gulf of Mexico (Olmecs, Huastecs and Totonacs), Maya, northern desert cultures, and finally Occidente (the western cultures of Nayarit, Jalisco, and Colima). A first-time visit may prove confusing, but after visiting some of the archaeological sites covered, the museum collection becomes far more relevant and illuminating.

Highlights include the giant Toltec *Atlante* statue in the Sala de Tula, the Aztec Calendar stone in the spectacular Sala México, and a huge Olmec head from San Lorenzo. Other notable exhibits are the superb Olmec *luchador* (wrestler), the Mayan mask of the Sun God, reproductions of Mayan murals from Bonampak, and a reconstruction of King Pakal's tomb from Palenque.

✚ 32A2

✉ Paseo de la Reforma, corner Gandhi, Bosque de Chapultepec

☎ (55) 5553 6386 /6381

🕐 Tue–Sun 9–7

🍴 Café ($) off courtyard

Ⓜ Chapultepec

✋ Moderate

❓ Guided tours, audio-guides, bookshop

One of the museum's treasures: a monumental Olmec head carved out of basalt

7
Palenque

The unique four-storey tower of the Palacio rises out of luxuriant vegetation

Deep in the rainforest of Chiapas stands this superb Maya site, both evocative and historically significant.

✚ 73E1

☎ (916) 345 0356/0211

🕐 Daily 8–5

🍴 Cafeteria ($) in museum

🚌 *Collectivo* bus to site from Calle Allende, Palenque

✈ Airstrip

ℹ Tourist office: Avenida Juárez, corner Absolo, Palenque

♿ Few

✋ Expensive; free Sun

↔ San Cristóbal (➤ 79), Tuxtla (➤ 80)

Palenque was founded in AD 615 by the great Mayan king Pakal, who set out to create a new architectural style, offering more light and harmonious, well-balanced spaces. At the center of the main site stands the Palacio (palace), a large complex of courtyards, corridors and tunnels crowned by a tiered tower that was probably an observatory. The entire structure is decorated with relief carvings, stucco friezes, and carved stelae.

Virtually opposite towers the Templo de las Inscripciones (Temple of Inscriptions), where steep steps rise to a summit temple then descend into the extraordinary tomb of King Pakal. Over 620 hieroglyphic inscriptions (including the date of 692) are surrounded by rich stucco decoration. Pakal's carved sarcophagus remains in the crypt but his fabulous jewelry is now at Mexico City's Anthropological Museum (➤ 21). Temple XIII, immediately to the west, has recently revealed the entombed body of the Reina Roja (red queen), adorned with fine jade ornaments that are at the site museum.

Across a stream on the hillside is a group of four beautiful temples. Some distance north lies another distinct group where a ball court fronts the Templo del Conde (Count's Temple). From here a path leads along the stream through jungle and past unexcavated structures to the main road and the museum and crafts shop.

8
Taxco

Taxco boasts a spectacular natural setting high in pine-clad mountains and some impressive colonial extravaganzas.

Taxco, a former staging-post on the royal road south to the port of Acapulco, developed considerably in the 18th century thanks to the enterprising French mining magnate José de la Borda, who left his mark both here and in Cuernavaca. A subsequent long and somnolent period ended in the 1930s when the American William Spratling regenerated the silver industry.

Red-roofed, whitewashed houses tumbling down the slopes line a maze of crooked cobblestoned streets winding uphill from the main road to the Plaza Borda. This social and commercial hub is overshadowed by the magnificent church of **Santa Prisca** (1759), a baroque masterpiece that was entirely financed by Borda. No expense was spared; its ornately carved facade and towers house a dazzling interior lined with 12 gilded altar-pieces, oil paintings and a monumental organ.

On a tiny plaza behind the church, the Museo Guillermo Spratling exhibits pre-Hispanic artifacts and replicas. A few twisting steps downhill from here stands a museum honoring another of Taxco's illustrious foreign residents, the German explorer Baron von Humboldt, who lived here in 1803. His mansion now houses the Museo de Arte Virreinal, a beautifully presented collection of colonial art with some exceptional pieces. There are numerous other fine mansions and churches to be explored, and a lively market area in the streets below Santa Prisca, packed with silver stores, offers the joys of hard bargaining.

Finally, for panoramic views of the town from the summit of Monte Taxco, take the *teleférico* (cable-car) from Los Arcos, located on the main access road.

Looking out over the rooftops of Taxco

🔟 72C2

ℹ️ Avenida de los Plateros 1 ☎ (762) 622 2274

♿ Few

🖐 Free

↔️ Cuernavaca (► 42), Acapulco (► 62)

❓ Easter Week processions peaking on Easter Fri

Parroquía de Santa Prisca

✉️ Plaza Borda

☎ (762) 662 0183

🕐 Mon–Sat 6AM–8PM, Sun 5:30AM–9PM

🍴 Cafés and restaurants ($) on square

9
Teotihuacán

✚ 42C2

☎ (55) 5956 0052

🕐 Daily 7AM–6PM

🍴 Restaurant ($) opposite the Citadel

🚌 Pirámides' bus from Terminal Tapo

Ⓜ San Lázaro

ℹ SECTUR: Avenida Presidente Mazariyk 172, Polanco, Mexico City

✋ Moderate; free Sun

❓ Guided tours from Mexico City (through hotels, travel agents)

Long before the Aztecs established their capital in central Mexico, Teotihuacán was the dominant center.

Located about one hour's drive from Mexico City, the archaeological site of Teotihuacán ("place of the dead") rises out of dry scrub and cacti. This once magnificent city, that covered over 20sq km (8sq miles) and sustained some 85,000 inhabitants at its zenith, evolved over a period of eight centuries before its destruction in around AD 750. Controversial 20th-century excavations and restoration of about 80 percent of the structures highlight Teotihuacán's ambitious building, carving and mural techniques.

The site lies a few degrees off a north–south axis traced by the Avenue of the Dead, that ends at the magnificent Pirámide de la Luna (Pyramid of the Moon). At the southern end is the vast Citadel, a walled quadrangle with the Temple of Quetzalcóatl against the eastern wall. This astonishing stepped construction (around AD 200), later built over, honors the plumed serpent (Quetzalcóatl) and the rain god (Tláloc) with 366 stone carvings.

Further north looms the gigantic Pirámide del Sol (Pyramid of the Sun) and, in its southern shadow, a dramatically designed and enlightening new museum displaying priceless exhibits and a huge scale model of the site, crossed by a transparent walkway. At the northwest end of the avenue, flanking another large ceremonial area, stands the extensively restored Palacio de Quetzalpapálotl, part of the priests' residential complex. Here, on an elevated patio, are square columns carved with bird and butterfly designs and remnants of red wall friezes. More patios and lower chambers show depictions of the jaguar god, conch shells and birds. A climb to the summit of the Pirámide de la Luna offers a final, sweeping view of this once great city.

Walk in the shadows of an exceptional civilisation and see fabulous carvings at the Templo de Quetzalcóatl (inset)

10
Xochimilco

42C1

Tren Ligero: La Noria, from Tasqueña

Fixed boat prices at Embarcadero

Few

Moderate

Museo Anáhuacalli (► 35)

Two-hour tours available (in Spanish) of Parque Ecológico ☎ (55) 5673 8061/7890 or in English through travel agents

Museo Dolores Olmedo Patiño

Avenida México 5843, La Noria

(55) 5555 1221/0891

Tue–Sun 10–6 except 25 Dec, 1 Jan and Easter Sun

Pleasant open-air café ($)

Brilliantly painted punts await the festive Sunday hordes

Xochimilco is a throwback to the capital's Aztec origins, with its canals and "floating" nursery gardens.

On the far southern edge of Mexico City, weekends are an excuse for feasting on fresh air while cruising the verdant canals of Xochimilco to the strident tunes of *mariachis*. Brilliantly decorated, pole-propelled *trajineras* (Mexican gondolas), packed with large groups or families, combine with countless flower- and food-sellers in canoes to create watery traffic jams. But this is Mexico, and chaos is part of the colorful picture.

The tradition of "floating" gardens goes back to the Aztecs, who, due to a shortage of farmland, devised a method of creating islands rooted by willow trees. These *chinampas* were used to grow fruit, vegetables and flowers to supply Tenochtitlán, the capital.

Xochimilco covers an area of 135sq km (52sq miles) that includes the town itself, with its beautiful 16th-century church of San Bernardino de Siena, beside several others, an archaeological museum, and the Parque Ecológico, an extensive area of grasslands, lagoons and canals. This is an ideal destination for birdwatchers, families or anyone desperate for unpolluted air close to the city center.

Xochimilco's final offering is a fascinating private **museum** housed in an atmospheric 400-year-old hacienda. The vast landscaped grounds are an added draw. Named after its owner, Dolores Olmedo, the museum exhibits an important collection of paintings by Diego Rivera and his wives, Frida Kahlo and Angelina Beloff, as well as pre-Hispanic artifacts (some probably copies) and an impressive collection of folk art.

What to See

Above: *ponchos for sale*
Right: *a Chamulan in Chiapas*

Tijuana Mexicali San Luis
Rio Colorado
Tecate
Ensenada
Puerto Peñasco Agua Prieta Ciudad
Juárez
Nogales Nuevo
Casas Grandes
San Felipe Casas
Grandes
El Rosario
Bahía
Kino Chihuahua
Hermosillo
Bahía de los Ángeles
Pinturas Rupestres Guaymas
Punta Guerrero
Eugenia Negro Cuauhtémoc
Laguna Ojo San Ignacio Ciudad Creel
de Liebre Obregón Barranca Ciudad
Santa Rosalía del Cobre Jiménez Moncl
Laguna
San Ignacio Mulegé Hidalgo
del Parral
El Fuerte
Loreto Tepehuanes
Los Mochis
Torreón
San Carlos Santiago
Bahía Magdalena Papasquiaro
Isla Culiacán Durango
Magdalena
La Paz San José
del Cabo
Mazatlán Zacatecas
Cabo Cabo San Lucas
San Lucas (Los Cabos) Acaponeta
Aguascalientes
Islas Tepic Leó
Marías
Guadalajara Irapua
Puerto Vallarta L de Chapala Zamo
Cabo Corrientes
Autlán de Morel
Navarro Colima
Uruapan
Manzanillo Presa del
Infiernillo
Ixtapa
Zihuatane

El Colorado
Baja
Golfo
Sonora
Sierra
Madre
Occidental
de
California (Mar de Cortés)
California
Bravo del Norte
Grande
Conchos
Grande
Sierra Madre
Grande de Santiago

0   200   400   600   800 km
0   100   200   300   400   500 miles

A   B   C

MEXICO

USA

Ciudad Acuña
Piedras Negras
Sabinas
Nuevo Laredo
Reynosa
Monterrey
Matamoros
Saltillo
Ciudad Victoria
Matehuala
Ciudad Mante
Tampico
Cabo Catoche
Río Lagartos
Cancún
Progreso
San Luis Potosí
Ciudad Valles
Mérida
Vallanolid
Poza Rica
Celestún
Chichén Itzá
Isla Cozumel
Querétaro
Uxmal
CIUDAD DE MÉXICO
Pachuca
El Tajín
Jalapa
Campeche
Yucatán
5700m
Citlaltépetl
Veracruz
Bahía de Campeche
Escárcega
Chetumal
Toluca
Puebla
Córdoba
Alvarado
Laguna de Catemaco
Cuernavaca
Izúcar de Matamoros
Huajapan de León
Minatitlán
Villahermosa
BH
Balsas
Chilpancingo
Tuxtepec
Palenque
Sierra Madre del Sur
Monte Albán
Oaxaca
Matías Romero
Tuxtla Gutiérrez
GCA
Acapulco
Juchitán
Puerto Escondido
Golfo de Tehuantepec
HONDURAS
Tapachula
ES

D
E
F

Pink flamingos are a familiar sight at Celestún, southwest of Mérida

Central Mexico

Central Mexico is the volcano-studded heart of the nation's colonial heritage. It was the silver mines of Zacatecas and Guanajuato that financed countless cathedrals in Spain, while a stream of baroque masterpieces was created in a roll-call of towns from Cuernavaca to Querétaro, Morelia and Puebla.

For today's conquistadores, this is not only one of the most culturally rewarding regions, where interest ranges from local craft specialties to exceptionally designed museums and dramatic archaeological sites, but it also offers spectacular scenery, lakes, forests, and generally cooler temperatures. Political events have marked this region—Morelia was the birthplace of José María Morelos, one of the leaders of the Independence movement, and the state of Morelos was the battleground of Emiliano Zapata, the revolutionary hero.

> *"And when we saw all those cities and villages built in the water, and other great towns on dry land... (it) seemed like an enchanted vision from the tale of Amadis "*.
>
> BERNAL DÍAZ
> *The Conquest of New Spain* (1568)

———————●———————

Papier-mâché skeletons are a common sight during Day of the Dead celebrations

CENTRAL MEXICO CITY

Casa los Mascarones

RIBERA DE SAN COSME

Parque Plaza Grijalva

Jardín del Arte

Monumento a Cuauhtémoc

PRESIDENTE MAZARYK

PLAZA MELCHOR OCAMPO

Monumento a la Independencia (El Ángel)

Museo de Cera

Museo Nacional de Antropología

Museo Rufino Tamayo

Información Turística

Zona Rosa

Jardín Botánico Parque Zoológico

Museo de Arte Moderno

L. Chapultepec

Bosque de Chapultepec

Monumento a los Niños Héroes

PASEO DE LA REFORMA

PLAZA RÍO DE JANEIRO

PLAZA MIRAVALLE

Castillo de Chapultepec y Museo Nacional de Historia

Museo del Caracol (Galería de Historia)

San Ángel Museo del Carmen Museo Frida Kahlo

Mexico City

Vibrant, ever-expanding and highly polluted, Mexico City is the political, cultural and economic heart of the country. Rimmed by volcanoes and lying at an altitude of 2,240m (7,350ft), Mexico's capital now claims over 20 million inhabitants. All of them surrender to the precariousness of living in a city that is sinking into the underground Lago de Texcoco, is plagued by crime and yet survived the terrible earthquake of 1985 with incredible civic solidarity. But despite all its negative factors, no one should pass up on a chance to spend a few days in this stimulating megalopolis.

Mexico City (Ciudad de México) can be divided into three main zones of interest—the Centro Histórico and Alameda area; the Zona Rosa and Chapultepec; and, far to the south, San Angel, Coyoacán, and Xochimilco. From Aztec ruins to impressive colonial edifices interspersed with modern blocks and wide boulevards, it presents strong visual contrasts. And between these facades cruises a stream of traffic, monopolized by the ubiquitous Volkswagen "beetles", the mainstay of the taxi business. In the Centro Histórico, pedicabs have been introduced, offering an alternative, more leisurely form of transport, while the excellent metro system covers the entire city.

Finding your way round can be tiring and frustrating, but the streets, alive with color, noise, and activity, more than compensate for this.

Flowers and food for sale on Xochimilco's waterways

What to See in Mexico City

BOSQUE DE CHAPULTEPEC (CHAPULTEPEC PARK)

This extensive park marks the western limits of the city center and is a favorite with some half-a-million city dwellers for weekend walks, picnics, and spontaneous open-air entertainment. Lakes, woods, lawns, museums, an amusement park, a zoo, and restaurants are among its diverse offerings. An entire day can easily be spent here.

Crowning the hill is the Castillo de Chapultepec, an austere construction dating from 1785 that now houses the **Museo Nacional de Historia**. Here, a rather dusty display covers Mexican history, and there are murals and the sumptuous royal apartments of the hapless Emperor Maximilian and his wife, Carlota. Don't miss the sweeping views from the terrace café. The castle is reached by a winding path from the Monumento a los Niños Heroes (Monument to the Young Heroes), at the main park entrance, which passes the snail-like Museo del Caracol (covering Independence and the Revolution) on the way.

The star of Chapultepec is the Museo Nacional de Antropología (► 21), located on the busy Paseo de la Reforma that slices across the park. Nearby are two major art museums—the Museo de Arte Moderno, and the Museo Rufino Tamayo (which concentrates on temporary exhibitions of contemporary art). Further west lies the Jardín Botánico, boating lakes, and restaurants, a high-tech children's museum, Museo Papalote (► 110), an amusement park, and the zoo that claims to be the world's oldest, as it existed during Aztec rule.

CATEDRAL METROPOLITANA (METROPOLITAN CATHEDRAL)

Dominating the Zócalo, Mexico City's main historic square, is this massive cathedral (Latin America's largest), which was begun in 1563, although its baroque facade dates from 1681 and the asymmetrical towers and dome were

---

32A1

Museo Nacional de Historia
- ☎ (55) 5241 3114
- 🕐 Tue–Sun 9–4:15
- 🍴 Café ($) on premises
- Ⓜ Chapultepec
- ♿ Few
- 🎟 Cheap; free Sun

Chapultepec's monument to the heroic army cadets, martyred during the Mexican–American War

---

33F3
- ✉ Zócalo, Centro Histórico
- 🕐 Daily 8–8
- 🍴 Cafés ($) on main square
- Ⓜ Zócalo ♿ Good
- 🎟 Free

34

added in 1813. The walls incorporate stones from the ruins of the Aztec Temple of Quetzalcóatl, but far more visible is the gilded baroque of the Capilla de Los Reyes (Chapel of the Kings) that glows in the gloomy interior. Subsidence is an ongoing problem—note the slope from high altar to the entrance—and metal structural supports are unfortunately highly visible. Next door stands the Churrigueresque-style El Sagrario (The Sacred), currently closed, with a remarkably ornate facade dating from 1760.

The Catedral Metropolitana, built over a period of 250 years, looms over the historic heart of the city

MUSEO ANÁHUACALLI (HOUSE OF ANÁHUAC) ✪✪✪

This outstanding museum is unfortunately located on the far southern edge of Coyoacán and requires some effort to visit. Conceived by the famous muralist and artist Diego Rivera, it embodies his identification with Mesoamerican culture. The pyramidal lava-stone structure houses his collection of 60,000 pre-Hispanic artifacts and a studio where he worked briefly before his death in 1957, leaving some unfinished paintings. Dark, labyrinthine corridors with onyx windows, stone ceiling mosaics, open terraces, arches, and stepped, altar-like displays all echo pre-Hispanic forms.

➕ 33F1
✉ Calle del Museo 150, San Pablo de Tepetlapa
☎ (55) 5617 4310
🕐 Tue–Sun 10–6. Closed Holy Week
🚇 Taxqueña, then taxi
♿ None
🎫 Moderate; free Sun

Brightly decorated mask on show in the Museo Anáhuacalli

35

A Walk through San Angel

A wander through the relaxed neighborhood of San Angel, along tree-lined cobbled streets, takes in ancient churches, museums, and shops.

From the San Angel pesero bus terminal walk up Avenida Revolución to the Museo del Carmen (► opposite) on your right. After visiting this monument, cross the avenue to the Centro Cultural and walk along Calle Madero to Plaza San Jacinto, lined with shops and restaurants.

On the right-hand side, the 18th-century Casa del Risco offers an unusual ceramic and shell-encrusted fountain, while inside it displays 16th- to 18th-century Mexican and European art. Next door is the Bazar del Sábado, a large crafts market open only on Saturdays. On the far corner of the plaza stands the beautiful 16th-century church and former monastery of San Jacinto.

The attractive church of San Jacinto stands in a peaceful walled garden

Continue along this street, past the crossroads, when it becomes Calle Miguel Hidalgo. At the 17th-century Casa Blanca turn right into Licenciados, following it downhill into Calle Leandro Valle.

These quiet streets offer a classic vision of Mexico City's wealthier residences, often brightly painted and set behind high walls, in a wide range of architectural styles.

At the main crossroads cross Altavista, passing a beautiful 18th-century hacienda on your left (now the San Angel Inn). Opposite stands the Museo Estudio Diego Rivera.

This blue structure was designed in 1930 for Rivera and includes a smaller, adjoining structure intended for Frida Kahlo. Rivera's studio, where he died in 1957, gives a fascinating insight into his last years.

Walk east down Altavista to Avenida Revolución and the Museo de Arte Carrillo Gil opposite, before returning south to the bus terminal.

Distance
About 3km (2 miles)

Time
2–3 hours, depending on stops

Start/end point
San Angel bus terminal
 32C1

Lunch
San Angel Inn ($$$)
 32C1
✉ Calle Diego Rivera 50
☎ (55) 5616 0537
(reservations essential)

MUSEO DEL CARMEN (CARMEN MUSEUM) ✪✪

On the edge of the delightful residential area of San Angel, in a cloistered garden, is this former Carmelite monastery, built in 1617 with tiled domes. The attractive, unusual interior encompasses floral friezes, wood and gesso ceiling reliefs, tiles, and frescos. Displayed throughout the former chapels and cells is an important collection of baroque religious art and, in the crypt, a somewhat ghoulish line-up of mummies.

✚ 32C1
✉ Avenida Revolución 4, corner Calle Monasterio, San Angel
☎ (55) 5550 1848
⏱ Tue–Sun 10–5
🍴 Cafés/restaurants ($–$$) on Plaza San Jacinto
🚌 San Angel *pesero* bus down Insurgentes
✋ Moderate

MUSEO FRANZ MAYER (FRANZ MAYER MUSEUM) ✪✪✪

Opened in 1986 in a superbly restored 16th-century mansion, this museum contains an exceptional collection of 16th- to 19th-century fine and applied arts, amassed by German immigrant and construction magnate, Franz Mayer. Influences and contrasts are highlighted between Asian, Arab, European, and Mexican styles, and priceless exhibits include paintings by Velázquez, Rivera, and Zubarán. Inlaid furniture, tapestries, silver and gold objects, wooden sculptures, glass, and ceramics complete this impressive collection.

✚ 33E3
✉ Avenida Hidalgo 45, Colonia Guerrero
☎ (55) 5518 2266
⏱ Tue–Sun 10–5
🍴 Excellent Café del Claustro ($)
🚇 Hidalgo, Bellas Artes
♿ Good
✋ Moderate

MUSEO FRIDA KAHLO (FRIDA KAHLO MUSEUM) ✪✪✪

Deep indigo and red-ochre walls picked out with brilliant green window-frames announce the eclectic and flamboyant tastes of Mexico's foremost woman artist, Frida Kahlo (► 14). Located in the pretty tree-lined streets of Coyoacán, where she spent most of her life, her family home reflects her wide-ranging interests and obsessions, and includes some poignant items such as the wheelchair to which she was confined in her last years, her four-poster bed and her last, unfinished painting (a portrait of Stalin). Beside these is a wealth of memorabilia in which Kahlo's husband, Diego Rivera, figures strongly, alongside her collections of masks, Teotihuacán sculptures, ex-votos, glass, lacquerware, and ceramics.

✚ 32C1
✉ Calle Londres 247, Coyoacán
☎ (55) 5554 5999
⏱ Tue–Sun 10–6
🍴 Cafés, restaurants ($–$$) on Jardín Centenario
🚌 General Anaya, then taxi
♿ Few
✋ Moderate

A 1930s self-portrait by Frida Kahlo, aged 23, prefigures her increasingly morbid later works

MUSEO NACIONAL DE ANTROPOLOGÍA (► 21, TOP TEN)

PALACIO DE BELLAS ARTES (PALACE OF FINE ARTS) ✪✪✪

Another of Mexico City's architectural showstoppers presides over the lively park, Alameda Central, on the western edge of the Centro Histórico. The Bellas Artes is a popular cultural center, with excellent temporary exhibitions, a theater where the renowned Ballet Folklórico performs, a large bookshop, gift shop, restaurant and a display of murals by the "big three"—Rivera, Orozco and Siqueiros—alongside Tamayo, on the upper floors. Set around a vast marble-lined atrium, the interior is pure art deco, in total contrast to the exuberant domed and colonnaded exterior.

PALACIO NACIONAL (NATIONAL PALACE) ✪✪

Mexico's first parliament is housed within this vast edifice flanking the eastern side of the *Zócalo*. The 17th-century palace replaced two previous ones, and is still the political powerhouse of Mexico as it holds the offices of the President, the National Archives and the Federal Treasury. Above the main entrance hangs the highly symbolic "Freedom Bell" that rang out in the town of Dolores, on 15 September 1810 to announce the fight for Independence. This is rung annually on the eve of Independence Day by the President to teeming masses gathered in the square.

Inside the courtyard a grand staircase leads up past extensive murals by Rivera, a *tour de force* that covers the history of Mexico. It is well worth following a guide to have the endless details explained. A small museum on the second floor, dedicated to Mexico's most revered president, Benito Juárez, is being renovated.

✚ 33E3
✉ Corner Avenida Juárez and Eje Central, Centro
☎ (55) 5512 2593
🕐 Palace: daily 10–6; museum: Tue–Sun 10–6
🍴 Café del Palacio ($$)
Ⓜ Bellas Artes
♿ Very good, except front steps
✋ Free
❓ Ballet Folklórico: Wed, Sun mornings and Sun evenings

✚ 33F2
✉ Zócalo
☎ (55) 5542 0606
🕐 Daily 9–5
🍴 Cafés ($) on Zócalo
Ⓜ Zócalo
♿ Good
✋ Free, but bring identification
🔁 Catedral Metropolitana (► 34), Templo Mayor (► opposite)
❓ Military lowering of flag daily before sunset with brass band

The ornate Bellas Artes combines architectural styles from 1900 to 1934

TEMPLO MAYOR (GREAT TEMPLE) ★★★

On the northeastern corner of the *Zócalo* is one of the few Aztec sites that remain. When it was completed in 1487, the temple consisted of seven superimposed structures, each one involving a four-day dedication ceremony and several thousand sacrificial victims. It was unearthed by accident in 1978 during construction of the metro. Four years of excavations uncovered hundreds of superb sculptures, now housed in an impressive modern museum behind the site, designed to resemble the temple layout.

Visitors can wander through the temple ruins on raised walkways that give close-ups on the altars devoted to Tláloc, the god of rain, and Huitzilopochtli, the fearsome god of war, along with replicas of sculptures. Highly visible is the wall of skulls standing in front of the museum, while inside, one of the most outstanding exhibits is a huge carved stone disc depicting the dismembered goddess of the moon, Coyolxauhqui.

TORRE LATINOAMERICANA ★
(LATIN-AMERICAN TOWER)

This lofty downtown landmark was the capital's first skyscraper when completed in 1956, but has since been surpassed by others. Towering 139m (456ft), it survived the 1985 earthquake and other tremors due to ingenious anti-seismic foundations that incorporate 361 concrete stilts. Today, it offers the best vantage point for views over the city (on rare, smogless days), particularly breathtaking at night. On the 44th floor is an outdoor viewing deck.

XOCHIMILCO (➤ 26, TOP TEN)

33F3
Seminario 8, Centro
(55) 5542 4943
Tue–Sun 9–5
Cafés and restaurants ($–$$) in and near *Zócalo*
Zócalo
Very good in museum, not on site
Cheap; free Sun
Palacio Nacional (➤ opposite), Catedral Metropolitana (➤ 34)

A serpent's head—one of many Aztec sculptures unearthed at the Templo Mayor

33E2
Corner Avenida Madero and Lázaro Cárdenas
(55) 5512 0844
Daily, 9:30AM–10:30PM
Cafés and restaurants ($–$$) in Centro Histórico
Bellas Artes, San Juan de Letrán
Moderate

Food & Drink

Mexican cuisine combines traditional indigenous recipes and ingredients with Spanish and North American influences. As varied as the country's scenery, the food of Mexico covers every budget, from street-corner *tacos* to sophisticated dishes that are reverting to pre-Hispanic recipes after decades of "international" cuisine.

Flipping fresh tortillas *at a roadside stall to provide the Mexican staple diet*

National Snacks

Corn *tortillas* have been the staff of life for centuries, and still accompany most dishes, while *tacos* and *burritos* are stuffed versions that make filling snacks. Less flavorsome wheat *tortillas* are now making inroads in the north, while dark-blue or red versions are made from special types of corn. The ubiquitous *tacos*, sold on every street of the country, are crisp fried *tortillas* stuffed with a fantastic variety of fillings and often topped with grated cheese. If you are careful about where you buy them, *tacos* make delicious and very cheap appetizers. In the south, *tamales* enter the field. These are similar, except that the ingredients are wrapped and steamed in corn husks or banana leaves and may sometimes be sweet. Further variations on the *tortilla* theme include *enchiladas* (cheese or chicken *tacos* baked in a spicy sauce) and *quesadillas*, mainly cheese-filled *tortillas*. A common accompaniment to the above is *frijoles*, red beans in a mushy sauce.

Timing

To get the most out of Mexican cuisine, follow the Mexican's rhythm. This entails large breakfasts that include fresh fruit and eggs—try *huevos rancheros*, fried eggs and diced chilli in a tomato sauce atop a *tortilla*. Mexican coffee, apart from in the coffee-growing region of Veracruz, is generally a diluted affair, so real *aficionados* should order espresso, Italian-style coffee is available in most upscale restaurants. Tea is also a pale imitation of the real thing, but Mexicans make up for this with a fantastic selection of fresh fruit juices (*jugos de frutas*), and you can order your own combination.

The main meal in Mexico is lunch, eaten at any time between 2 and 5PM, when restaurants offer good-value set menus (*comidas corridas*). Dinner, if taken at all, is generally after 9PM. Tourists who may not want a large lunch will find that resorts cater for European eating hours, but if you travel off the beaten track you will only find upscale restaurants open in the evenings.

Essential ingredients for the ritual of tequila drinking—squeezed lime, salt and the elixir itself

Seafood

Mexican seafood is obviously best along the coast, and resorts cook up exceptionally fresh fish such as *huachinango* (red snapper), *robalo* (snook) and prawn dishes (*camarones*). However, be warned, *sopa de camarón* is one of Mexico's spiciest dishes. Freshwater fish includes *pescado blanco*, a delicate white fish from Lago de Pátzcuaro, and *langostino*, a large crayfish usually cooked *al mojo de ajo*. This popular seafood preparation consists of fried garlic—again, be warned!

Guacamole may have traveled the world, but its original Mexican version is unbeatable

41

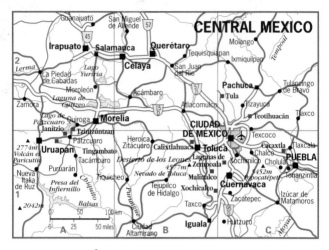

What to See in Central Mexico

CHOLULA ★

Once a major ceremonial town dedicated to Quetzalcóatl, Cholula suffered extensive destruction by Cortés' army on its march to Mexico City. Numerous shrines and churches include the Convento Franciscano (1549) and the 18th-century Capilla Real with its 49 domes. The **Gran Pirámide**, the largest pyramid in the Americas, dominates this otherwise nondescript town. Crowning the summit is the 16th-century Templo de Nuestra Señora de los Remedios (Temple of Our Lady of Remedies), while below, some 8km (5 miles) of tunnels have revealed extensive remains of murals. A small museum near the tunnel entrance houses copies of the frescos.

CUERNAVACA ★★

Often dubbed the "city of eternal spring," Cuernavaca is a favorite bolt-hole for the capital's wealthier inhabitants. Despite a population of over one million, and the largest number of swimming pools per capita in the world, it has a delightful center, and, situated only 65km (40 miles) south of Mexico City, makes an attractive alternative base. Two adjoining plazas form the heart of town, over which looms the **Palacio de Cortés** (1530), a massive fortress-palace housing a fascinating museum of regional archaeology, colonial history, and the Revolution. There is also a masterful mural by Diego Rivera depicting Spanish oppression of the indigenous peoples.

In front lie the plazas, focal points for a crafts market, promenading, and general festivities. A short walk west up Calle Hidalgo brings you to the magnificent Catedral (1530), built by the Franciscans. Despite being one of

---

+ 42C1

ℹ Opposite main entrance

⟷ Puebla (► 48)

? Guides available to explore main tunnel

Gran Pirámide

✉ Highway 190, Cholula

⏰ Daily 9–5

🍴 Restaurant Choloyán ($), Avenida Morelos

♿ Few

💲 Moderate; free Sun

+ 42C1

ℹ Avenida Morelos Sur 802, Colonia La Palma
☎ (777) 318 7561

Palacio de Cortés

✉ Avenida Benito Juárez

☎ (777) 312 8171

⏰ Tue–Sun 9–6

🍴 Restaurants and cafés ($–$$) on the zócalo

♿ Good (ground floor only)

💲 Moderate

Mexico's oldest churches, its interior is strikingly modern. Across Avenida Morelos is the Jardín Borda, a beautiful landscaped garden surrounding a mansion (1783) built by French silver magnate José de la Borda. It was once a favorite retreat for Emperor Maximilian. Historical documents, folk art, and temporary art shows are among the exhibits.

GUADALAJARA

Mexico's second-largest city offers a compact historical center, a pleasant climate and lively traditions from *mariachis* to glass-blowing. The monuments are dotted around four central plazas surrounding the Catedral, a massive edifice that combines numerous architectural styles due to repeated reconstruction. Flanking the Plaza de Armas outside is the Palacio Nacional, where Miguel Hidalgo declared an end to slavery, an event captured by Orozco's powerful murals on its walls.

Immediately north is the fascinating **Museo Regional de Jalisco** (1701) housed in a former seminary. Exhibits cover pre-Hispanic artifacts, religious and colonial paintings, decorative arts and handicrafts by Jalisco's Huichol and Cora Indians. To the east stands the neoclassical Teatro Delgollado, where Guadalajara's state

orchestra and Grupo Folklórico perform. From here, the Plaza Tapatía stretches east to the impressive Instituto Cultural Cabañas, which was designed as an orphanage in 1805. This is now the focal point for the city's cultural activities, as well as housing a homage to José Clemente Orozco, the city's renowned 20th-century painter, whose vigorous murals adorn the domed chapel.

Other offerings include a labyrinthine crafts and food market, the Mercado Libertad, and, nearby, the Plaza de los Mariachis, where cafés and restaurants are invaded by *mariachis* daily.

Not to be missed are the villages of Tlaquepaque and Tonalá, now engulfed by the urban sprawl. Tlaquepaque makes a colorful outing by bus from the center. Elegant 19th-century mansions converted into restaurants and crafts boutiques radiate from the Jardín Hidalgo and El Parián. The latter is a remodeled structure housing more crafts shops and restaurants. In a short distance lies Tonalá, with its glass and pottery workshops.

28C2

Plaza Tapatía, Morelos 102 ☎ (33) 3668 1600 or (800) 363 2200

Laguna de Chapala (► 44)

Museo Regional de Jalisco

Corner Avenida Hidalgo and Liceo

(33) 3614 9957

Tue–Sat 9–5:30, Sun 9–5

Cafés and restaurants ($) on plazas

Few

Moderate

The Palacio de Gobierno, built in 1751 on Guadalajara's Plaza de Armas, one of the four squares surrounding the Catedral

43

Olmec heads at Jalapa

🔶 29D2

ℹ️ Avenida Avila Camacho
191 ☎ (228) 842 1214

↔️ El Tajín (► 49)

Museo de Antropología

✉️ Avenida Xalapa, Estado
de Veracruz

☎ (228) 815 0920

🕐 Daily 9–5

🍴 Cafetería ($) in museum

♿ Excellent

🎟️ Moderate

🔶 28C2

✉️ 50km (31 miles)
southeast of Guadalajara,
40 minutes by car

🍴 Vast choice of cafés and
restaurants ($–$$$) along
northwest shore

ℹ️ Tourist office in
Guadalajara (► 43)

♿ Good

GUANAJUATO (► 18, TOP TEN)

JALAPA ⚪⚪

Blazing sun in the morning and cooler mists in the afternoon characterize Jalapa's picturesque location, high in the coffee-growing hills inland from Veracruz. On the horizon is the Cofre de Perote volcano (4,282m) overlooking this lively university town, with its atmospheric colonial heart of steep, winding streets, gardens, parks and grandiose administrative buildings. The star sight is the excellent **Museo de Antropología**, an imaginatively designed modern building at the northern end of town. Here sunlit patios and terraced marble halls opening on to a landscaped park display a collection of the pre-Hispanic cultures of the Gulf region. Giant basalt heads from the Olmec center of San Lorenzo vie with the wonderful "smiling" sculptures of the Totonacs at El Tajín and the superb pottery of the northern Huastecs.

LAGUNA DE CHAPALA ⚪

The warm climate of Mexico's largest natural lake has long attracted a stream of expatriates, from writers such as D. H. Lawrence and Sybille Bedford to today's 6,000 North American retirees. Sleepy fishing villages stud the lake shore, but the main animation is along the northwest shore at Chapala, Ajijic and Jocotepec. Boat trips visit the two islands of Los Alacranes and Mexcala, the former boasting the lake's most scenic fish restaurants. More authentic in style, and the source of colorful handwoven *serapes* (shawls), is Jocotepec.

MORELIA ✪✪

The uncontested architectural jewel of fertile Michoacán is its capital, Morelia, a dynamic yet compact university town. Although founded in 1541 as Valladolid, it was renamed Morelia at independence to honor Jose María Morelos, a native son and key figure in the movement. Dominating the central plaza is a massive pink-stone cathedral, said to be the third largest in the Americas. Harmonious arcades, churches, colleges, and imposing colonial buildings radiate from here and include the magnificent mansion that now houses the **Museo Regional Michoacán**, covering local ethnography, archaeology, and colonial history. One block north is Mexico's oldest university, the Colegio de San Nicolás, and a few steps further the superbly proportioned Palacio Clavijero.

🔲 42A2
ℹ️ Palacio Clavijero, Nigromante 79 ☎ (443) 312 8082
↔️ Pátzcuaro (► below)

Museo Regional Michoacán
✉️ Allende 305, corner of Abasolo
☎ (443) 312 0407
🕐 Tue–Sat 9–7, Sun 9–2. Closed 25 Dec, 1 Jan, Easter Sun
🍴 Cafés and restaurants ($) on square
♿ Good 🚻 Moderate

PÁTZCUARO ✪✪✪

Situated beside a tranquil lake, Pátzcuaro is an unusual and delightful little town. Quaint cobbled streets lined with neat whitewashed houses wind uphill from Plaza Vasco de Quiroga and Plaza Gertrudis Bocanegra to reach the Basílica de Nuestra Señora de la Salud. Founded in 1554 but rebuilt in 1883, the church contains a much revered corn-paste statue of the Virgin of Health, and on the eighth day of every month pilgrims flock here with requests. Close by is the **Museo de Artes Populares**, housed in a former college dating from 1540. Inside are displayed Michoacán's rich local crafts, from lacquerware to copper. Downhill from Plaza Gertrudis Bocanegra is the lake. From the main *embarcadero*, boats ferry visitors to the commercialized island of Janitzio. Crowning its hilltop is a gigantic statue of Morelos.

🔲 42A1
ℹ️ Plaza Vasco de Quiroga 50, Guion A ☎ (434) 342 1214
↔️ Morelia (► above)

Museo de Artes Populares
✉️ Enseñanza y Alcantarilla
☎ (434) 342 1029
🕐 Tue–Sat 9–7, Sun 9–3
🍴 Cafés and restaurants ($) on main plazas
♿ Good
🚻 Cheap

Morelos dominates the island of Janitzio

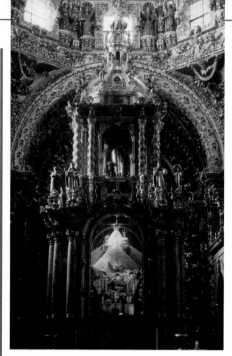

The dazzling Churrigueresque stucco work in Puebla's Capilla del Rosario took 40 years to complete

➕ 42C1

ℹ️ Avenida 5 Oriente
(southern side of
Catedral) ☎ (222) 246
2044/1285

Museo Amparo

✉️ Calle 2 Sur, corner
Avenida 9 Oriente
☎ (222) 229 3850
🕐 Wed–Mon 10–6
🍴 Cafés and restaurants ($)
on *zócalo*
♿ Few
💰 Moderate

PUEBLA ⊙⊙

Ringed by four volcanoes and less than two hours by road from the capital is Puebla, Mexico's fourth-largest city. Though very industrialized, it is surprisingly easy-going, and offers fabulous examples of baroque architecture, in particular the Templo de Santo Domingo. At the heart of this church is the Capilla del Rosario (1690), the most sumptuous Dominican construction in the world, where gilded and carved stucco blankets the dome and walls as a backdrop to a bejeweled figure of the Virgin.

The 17th-century Ex-Convento de Santa Rosa, now converted into the Museo de las Artesanías, houses the nuns' kitchens where it is said the famed Pueblan *mole* sauce was invented (➤ 93). Religious art is exhibited at the Ex-Convento de Santa Monica, full of disguised doorways and secret passageways, dating from 1857 when President Juárez closed all religious structures.

Flanking the south of the *zócalo* is the vast Catedral, a mixture of various styles due to its prolonged construction between 1575 and 1649. Three blocks southeast is the impressively designed **Museo Amparo**, successfully incorporating high-tech displays of archaeology and viceregal art into a converted 16th-century hospital. Puebla is noted for the Talavera tiles that adorn many facades or domes. Particularly exceptional is the Casa de Alfeñique, home to the Museo Regional, while at Uriarte (➤ 106) workshops still make this renowned decorative ceramic.

A Drive around Lake Pátzcuaro

Head out of Pátzcuaro on the road to the lake, then follow Highway 14 to Tzintzuntzán, about 20km (12 miles) away.

Above the town is Las Yacatas, a row of stepped, circular pyramids offering sweeping lake views and a small museum. In Tzintzuntzán itself stands the partly ruined 16th-century Templo de San Francisco. Close by are numerous craft outlets for local pottery, woodcarving, and straw figures.

Continue to Quiroga, the largest commercial town on the lake. Turn left at the main square for a short drive to Santa Fe de la Laguna.

It was here in the 1540s that Don Vasco de Quiroga, Michoacán's first bishop, attempted to set up a model community based on Thomas More's *Utopia*. The 16th-century hospital and chapel still stand and the village square has been completely renovated, together offering an unusual stop.

Continue to skirt the lake through pine forests to the promontory of Chupicaro.

Next stop is San Jerónimo, a sprawling lakeside village jutting out on a small promontory, where activities concentrate on woodcarving and boatbuilding.

Drive on about 15km (9 miles) to the neighboring villages of Puacuaro, Napizaro, and Erongaricuaro.

The pure Purepecha inhabitants of Puacuaro and Napizaro specialize in basket-making. In Erongaricuaro (meaning "look-out tower on the lake") visit the 16th-century Franciscan church and seminary. Handicrafts made here include inlaid furniture, weaving, and embroidery.

The road continues around the lake through San Francisco Uricho, Arocutín, Tocuaro, and San Pedro, before rejoining Highway 14 and returning to Pátzcuaro.

Las Yacatas, in Tzintzuntzán, were dedicated to Curicaveri, the Purepecha god of fire

Distance
About 65km (40 miles)

Time
Allow a leisurely day to include stops

Start/end point
Pátzcuaro
✚ 42A1

Lunch
Restaurants ($) at Chupicaro

47

✚ 42B2
ℹ Pasteur Norte 4 ☎ (442) 238 5000

Convento de Santa Cruz
✉ Avenida Independencia, corner Manuel Acuña
☎ (442) 238 5000
🕐 Mon–Fri 9–2, 5–8:30, Sat–Sun 11–6
🍴 Cafés and restaurants ($–$$) on Plaza de las Armas
♿ Few
💲 Donation. Guided tours

QUERÉTARO ✪✪

The prosperous, industrial town of Querétaro has a harder edge than its neighbors, yet despite this it is rich in history, with a wealth of baroque architecture and a monumental aqueduct (1735). From the central church of San Francisco, a well-designed pedestrianized area, dense with street stalls, leads uphill to the shady, porticoed Plaza de las Armas. This focal point for restaurants and shoe-shiners is the site of the 18th-century Government Palace, situated beside several imposing mansions.

Adjoining San Francisco in another former convent is the fabulous Museo Regional, with its renowned collection of viceregal paintings. Southwest from here are Querétaro's two baroque jewels, the Templo de Santa Clara (1633), with walls covered in high-relief altarpieces, and the equally magnificent Templo de Santa Rosa (1752).

East of San Francisco stands the church and former **Convento de Santa Cruz** (1654) that served as a prison to Emperor Maximilian before his execution in 1867.

✚ 42B2
ℹ Plaza Allende ☎ (415) 152 6565
🔁 Guanajuato (▶ 18)

Museo Regional
✉ Cuna de Allende 1
🕐 Tue–Sun 10–4. Closed 25 Dec, 1 Jan, Easter Sun
🍴 Cafés and restaurants ($–$$) on plaza and nearby
♿ Few
💲 Cheap

SAN MIGUEL DE ALLENDE ✪✪

This is central Mexico's "gringo" city, a small, picturesque town buzzing with US expatriates, students, and visitors. Reflecting this influx is a plethora of cafés, bars, restaurants, and stores geared to their needs. Rising above lively Plaza Allende are the lofty, neo-gothic spires of the Parroquía (1880), while across a side street stands the 18th-century birthplace of Ignacio Allende, an Independence protagonist. Now the **Museo Regional**, it illustrates the city's history and archaeology alongside contemporary art. Another impressive 18th-century mansion is the Casa del Mayorazgo, its restored interior now houses an art collection. This artistic theme continues in exhibitions at the Centro Cultural Ignacio Ramírez.

The fluted spires of the Parroquía soar above San Miguel, now designated a national monument

EL TAJÍN ✪✪✪

Set in lush, scenic hills are the magnificent ruins of the Totonac civilisation (4th–12th centuries). The nearest base is 12km (7 miles) away at Papantla, a pretty little town known for its vanilla plantations. El Tajín's main sight is the Pirámide de los Nichos (Pyramid of the Niches), a striking, tiered edifice incorporating 365 niches rising beside numerous other buildings and at least 10 ball courts. Here, opposing teams played out their ritual game, which ended in sacrifice. The main ball-court walls are carved with fine bas-reliefs depicting players, sacrifices, and *pulque*-drinking. Uphill lies El Tajín Chico, where more structures surround the Edificio de las Columnas, decorated with intricate stone mosaics. At the entrance, outside the excellent modern museum, a 30m pole is used by local *voladores* (flying dancers) to re-enact a dangerous but spectacular Totonac ritual.

✚ 29D2
✉ Highway 130, Estado de Veracruz (25km/15 miles southeast of Poza Rica)
☎ (784) 842 0026
🕐 Daily 9–5
🍴 Café ($) on site
♿ Moderate; free Sun

❓ *Voladores* perform at noon daily

TAXCO (► 23, TOP TEN)

TEOTIHUACÁN (► 24–5, TOP TEN)

Above: *Totonac voladores at El Tajín*
Right: *people-watching*

The North &
Baja California

Northern Mexico is the land of interminable desert rising abruptly into the Sierra Tarahumara and its canyons (▶ 16), while the coastlines are washed by the Pacific Ocean, the Mar de Cortés and, to the east, the Gulf of Mexico. Proximity to the U.S. has generated a string of unattractive industrialized border cities, but in the long finger of land known as Baja California lies a tempting variety of landscapes, from scenic sierra to spectacular, often deserted beaches. From its border town Tijuana to the southern cape is a distance of 1,200km (746 miles), but it is the southern half that offers most diversity. This is where whale-watching, birdwatching, sport fishing, scuba diving, riding, and trekking take over, backed up by still-fledgling coastal resorts that contrast with remote Jesuit missions in the sierra.

"It is known that to the right of the Indies there exists an island called California very near the terrestrial paradise".

GARCÍA DE MONTALVO
The Adventures of Esplandian
(1510)

───────●───────

A roadside shrine near La Paz echoes the form of the surrounding cacti

What to See in the North and Baja California

BAHÍA DE LOS ANGELES

28A4

Museo de Historia Natural
- Restaurants ($) nearby
- Good
- Cheap

This starkly beautiful bay on the Mar de Cortés makes a welcome change from the dry inland desert and is easily reached from the main highway, 68km (42 miles) away. Facilities include an airstrip, several good hotels, trailer parks, restaurants, and the **Museo de Historia Natural**. On the horizon lies Isla Angel de la Guarda, a large island reserve, while the waters of the bay are alive with dolphins, finback whales, and sea lions. Boat trips can be arranged.

BARRANCA DEL COBRE (➤ 16, TOP TEN)

LOS CABOS

www.visitloscabos.org

28B2

Edificio Fonatur, Muelle Turístico, Cabo San Lucas
☎ (114) 20446

Centro Cultural de Los Cabos
- Behind Presidente Forum Resort
- ☎ (866) LOSCABOS
- Tue–Sun 9–5, Wed 9–1
- Cafés and restaurants ($$) on Paseo Mijáres
- Good
- Cheap

At the tip of Baja lie the twin resorts of Cabo San Lucas and San José del Cabo, 30 minutes apart but with quite distinct atmospheres. Cabo San Lucas is a boisterous, expensive, modern golf resort while San José retains a quaint Mexican village atmosphere beneath its touristic veneer. Los Cabos offer luxury hotels, golf courses, sport fishing, surfing, scuba diving at the unique underwater sand cascades, whale-watching, and horse riding in the sierra.

San José dates back to 1730 when its Jesuit mission was founded. Adjacent Paseo Mijáres, with its stone and stucco 19th-century houses, is now the focal point for restaurants, bars, stores and real-estate agents. At the river estuary, a small **cultural center** displays arts and crafts, fossils, and reproduction cave-paintings, while next to this is an ecological reserve, home to 200 bird species.

The Baja peninsula ends at El Arco, a massive rock arch that terminates the headland. Boat trips from the marina visit this landmark and El Faro Viejo (Old Lighthouse), which offers panoramic views. Pelicans, seals, sea lions, dolphins, and whales can be seen, while underwater is a paradise for snorkelers and divers.

A heavily laden beach vendor at Cabo San Lucas

CASAS GRANDES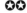

28B4

Zona Arqueológica de Paquimé, Casas Grandes
☎ (636) 692 4140
Tue–Sun 10–5
Cafeteria ($)
Cheap; free Sun

This is the most important archaeological site in northern Mexico, best reached from Ciudad Juárez. Thought to date from AD 1000, Casas Grandes was abandoned in the mid-14th century following attacks by Apaches. Structures on site include platforms, ball courts, underground chambers, and the remains of three-storey adobe houses. Excavations have unearthed rich finds of Paquimé pottery, necklaces of semi-precious stones, and carvings of Quetzalcóatl, some displayed in the museum.

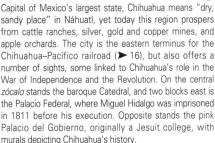

28C4

Libertad 1300, 1st floor, Edificio Agustín Melgar
☎ (614) 410 1077

Museo de la Revolución

✉ Calle Décima 3014
☎ (614) 416 2958
🕐 Tue–Sun 10–1, 3–7
🍽 None
♿ None
💵 Cheap

Chihuahua's cathedral was begun in 1726 but only completed in 1826

CHIHUAHUA ✪

Capital of Mexico's largest state, Chihuahua means "dry, sandy place" in Náhuatl, yet today this region prospers from cattle ranches, silver, gold and copper mines, and apple orchards. The city is the eastern terminus for the Chihuahua–Pacífico railroad (► 16), but also offers a number of sights, some linked to Chihuahua's role in the War of Independence and the Revolution. On the central *zócalo* stands the baroque Catedral, and two blocks east is the Palacio Federal, where Miguel Hidalgo was imprisoned in 1811 before his execution. Opposite stands the pink Palacio del Gobierno, originally a Jesuit college, with murals depicting Chihuahua's history.

South of the center are two major museums. The Museo Regional is housed in the Quinta Gameros, a lavishly decorated mansion displaying art nouveau kitsch and a display of Paquimé pottery from Casas Grandes. Four blocks south is the **Museo de la Revolución**, in the mansion where revolutionary leader Pancho Villa lived. Exhibits include photographs, arms, documents, and the black 1922 Dodge peppered with bullet holes in which Villa was assassinated.

28A4

Tourist and Convention Bureau, Lázaro Cárdenas, corner Miramar ☎ (646) 172 3022

Bodegas Santo Tomás

✉ Avenida Miramar 666
☎ (646) 178 3333
🕐 Daily tours at 11, 1, 3
♿ Few
💵 Moderate

ENSENADA ✪

Just over 100km (62 miles) south of Tijuana lies Ensenada, Baja California's most popular resort, receiving half a million visitors each year. These are mostly Californians on weekend drinking, eating, shopping, and sport fishing sprees, but during the week the town and its bay return to more tranquil fishing and shipping activities. Ultra-fresh seafood is available at the Mercado de Pescas opposite the pier, and local wine can be sampled at the wineries. The largest, **Bodegas Santo Tomás**, offers daily wine tastings in its converted warehouse.

South of town is La Bufadora, a blowhole where wave

action produces a dramatic geyser, and the secluded beach of Punta Banda. Nearby are the surfers' favorites of San Miguel, Tres Marías, California, and La Joya.

Historic national heroes are honored in Ensenada

GUERRERO NEGRO ✪

Although ostensibly a dull town of endless saltflats, vats, and warehouses, Guerrero Negro is also the entry point to the Laguna Ojo de Liebre (Scammon's Lagoon), a protected national park where grey whales come to breed between December and March. Lookout posts dot the shore and skiffs can be rented at the beach.

✚ 28A4
❓ Reserva de la Biosfera El Vizcaino ☎ (615) 157 1777/0177; Eco-Tours Malarrimo ☎ (615) 157 0100

> ### *Did you know ?*
> *From December to March, the warm lagoon waters of Ojo de Liebre and San Ignacio see the courting, mating and breeding of some 20,000 grey whales that swim south from the Bering Sea.*

HERMOSILLO ✪

The industrialized city of Hermosillo appears to have little charm, yet its strategic site, 225km (140 miles) south of the border town of Nogales on Highway 15, with access to the beach resorts of Guaymas and Bahía Kino, about 100km (62 miles) west, makes it a good stop-over. The attractive colonial heart centers around the shady Plaza de Zaragoza, flanked by the Catedral and the Palacio de Gobierno. South of here lies the Centro Ecológico de Sonora, a zoo and botanical garden full of indigenous and desert specimens.

On the slopes of the Cerro de la Campaña, a hill overlooking the town, is the **Museo Regional de Sonora** in a converted penitentiary and, further north, the Ciudad Universitario, with its museum of local sericulture.

✚ 28B4
ℹ️ Palacio de Gobierno, Edificio Norte, Paseo Río Sonora ☎ (800) 716 2555

Museo Regional de Sonora
✉️ Jesús García Finál, corner Estéban Sarmiento
☎ (662) 217 1241
🕐 Wed–Sat 10–5:30, Sun 10–3:30
💲 Moderate; free Sun

A Drive through Southern Baja

This drive circles the southern tip of Baja California, passing through dramatic sierra and tiny villages, with a night stop at Los Cabos.

From La Paz drive south on Highway 1 before taking the left fork at San Pedro. From here the road winds up to El Triunfo.

Rich silver veins were discovered here in 1862, leading to a population explosion till the mines closed down in 1926. The town is now virtually a ghost town though small-scale mining has resumed.

Whiling away the afternoon in the sleepy former silver-mining town of El Triunfo

Continue 8km (5 miles) to San Antonio, a farming and former silver-mining town, before twisting up into the Sierra El Triunfo. The road descends again to the coast at Los Barriles, renowned for its spectacular winds.

Stop here for a refreshing swim in the Bahía de las Palmas before lunch.

The road skirts the coast before twisting inland and climbing past small villages. About 4km (2.5 miles) beyond Santiago it crosses the Tropic of Cancer, marked by a concrete sphere. At Las Casitas, the road widens to descend to San José del Cabo (➤ 52), an ideal night–stop. Next morning, head for Cabo San Lucas along the coastal highway and drive to the marina.

Stop here for a glass-bottomed boat trip around the striking rock formation known as El Arco (The Arch).

Drive out of town on Highway 1 to Todos Santos, 80km (50 miles) to the north.

This quiet farming town is attracting a growing community of Americans and a small arts and crafts industry. Beautiful Playa Punta Lobos and Playa San Pedrito are east of town. From here, 80km (50 miles) brings you back to La Paz.

Distance
397km (247 miles)

Time
2 days

Start/end point
La Paz
➕ 28B3

Lunch
Hotel Palmas de Cortés ($$)
✉ Conocido en Los Barriles
☎ (624) 141 0050

The restored 1752 Jesuit church in Loreto has survived several earthquakes

LORETO

Loreto, the first capital of the Californias, has a population of only 9,000, making it a peaceful getaway in a beautiful setting, backed by the Sierra de la Giganta. The modest town center claims the well-conserved Jesuit mission, from where Father Junípero Serra set out in 1769 to establish a chain of 17 Californian missions. Inside, the **Museo de los Misiones** gives an informative introduction to local missionary activities. Around the church is a pedestrian area leading down to the harbor and beach where Loreto's few hotels are located. Activities include tennis at one of the world's most modern tennis centers, sport fishing, hiking, and scuba diving, as well as boat trips to the lovely Isla Coronado. A mega-resort is planned 20km (12 miles) south at Puerto Loreto.

🖪 28B3

Museo de los Misiones
✉ Salvatierra 16
☎ (613) 135 0005
🕐 Tue–Sun 9–6
🍴 Cafés ($) in nearby plaza
♿ Good
💲 Cheap

MULEGÉ

The sleepy oasis town of Mulegé overlooks the mouth of the 40km (25 mile) Bahía de Concepción, backed by the Sierra de Santa Lucía. The original settlement was founded beside Baja's only navigable river, whose water has nourished large groves of olive trees and date palms. On the hilltop above stands the 1705 Misión de Santa Rosalía, once an open prison and now the Museo de Mulegé, with an eclectic range of exhibits including old diving and mining equipment. Low-key Mulegé mainly attracts sport fishermen, but also offers kayaking upriver or to outlying islands, scuba diving, and jeep or horseback trips to see the Cuevas de San Borjita paintings.

🖪 28A3
❓ Kayaking and cave-painting tours through Hotel Hacienda, Calle Romero Rubio, Mulegé
☎ (800) 346 3942; fax: (615) 153 0021
💲 Moderate

🗺 28B3
ℹ️ Carretera al Norte Km 5.5
de Mayo
☎ (612) 122 5939.
Small office on Tourist
Wharf, Paseo Alvaro
Obregón 2130,
Mon–Sat

Museo de Antropología
✉️ Calle Altamirano corner 5
de Mayo
☎ (612) 122 0162
🕐 Mon–Fri 9–6
🍴 Cafés and restaurants ($)
on Plaza Constitución
♿ Few
🎟 Free

*Late afternoon sun floods
the beach, boats, and
malecón at La Paz*

LA PAZ ⬤⬤

The prosperous capital of Baja California Sur (south Baja), La Paz, lies on a large bay opening on to the Mar de Cortés, an ecologically rich gulf dotted with island nature reserves. Protected to the north by the peninsula of El Monogote, whose shores are increasingly targeted by resort hotels, downtown La Paz looks directly west across the bay. This provides a major natural feature—dramatic sunsets.

La Paz (ironically meaning "peace") suffered a turbulent past, set in motion by Hernán Cortés in 1535. Vicious conflicts with the indigenous inhabitants were exacerbated over the centuries by droughts, famines, smallpox, pirates, American troops during the Texan War and, in 1853, the infamous William Walker, intent on installing slavery. As a result, no indigenous groups survived in Baja. The town's fortunes were revived partly thanks to American sport fishermen, ferry services, the Transpeninsular highway and its free-port status, so that today La Paz boasts one of Mexico's highest per-capita incomes.

The center of La Paz radiates from Plaza Constitución, where the Palacio de Gobierno faces the picturesque 19th-century Catedral de la Señora de la Paz, built on the site of a 1720 mission. Close by is the Teatro de la Ciudad, where modern facilities include art galleries and a library. La Paz's history is covered at the **Museo de Antropología**, where informative displays illustrate Baja geology, the early Pericue, Cochimi and Guaicura inhabitants and information on the cave paintings near San Ignacio (➤ opposite).

The balmy climate averaging 25°C, constant breezes and scenic palm-fringed *malecón* (seafront promenade) make La Paz a relaxing base for exploring the inland sierra, indulging in endless watersports or boat trips, or enjoying the fine white sand of its beaches. The modernized town center has few historical sights, but Baja is, after all, about the great outdoors.

Although the primary winter (January–March) grounds for humpback whales are around Los Cabos, they sometimes venture into the Bay of La Paz. Year-round boat trips go to Isla Partida, a seal sanctuary, and the islands of Cerralvo and Espíritu Santo, both nature reserves that offer diving and swimming in the transparent waters of their coves. Sport fishing meanwhile takes advantage of the 850 species of fish in the warm waters of the gulf.

> ### *Did you know ?*
>
> *No fewer than 120 species of cactus inhabit the Baja landscape, from miniature cushions to gigantic 20m-high cardons. In March and April their upper branches blossom with white flowers. Also common are the organ-pipe cactus, mainly in southern Baja, and the barrel cactus, which can serve as an emergency water source.*

SAN FELIPE ✪
Running from the border town of Mexicali, Highway 5 ends at San Felipe, a fishing village that has now mushroomed into a resort. The main reason to come here is for the prolific fishing. San Felipe also attracts beach-lovers, as its golden sands border the warm Mar de Cortés (as opposed to the chillier and rougher Pacific). Impressive tides make the beach south of town a popular target for dune-buggying, and this is where an increasing number of upscale hotels are appearing.

✚ 28A4
ℹ Mar de Cortés corner Manzanillo ☎ (686) 577 1865 🕐 Tue–Sun 9–2, 4–6

SAN IGNACIO ✪✪
This attractive oasis town on the edge of the monotonous Desierto de Vizcaíno makes a tranquil stop-over as well as being the entry point to Laguna San Ignacio, a major whale-watching spot 70km (43 miles) away. The little town itself features a shady plaza, a mission church (1786), a small **ethnographic museum** and extensive date-palm groves planted by the Jesuits. Trips can be arranged to the lagoon during the whale season and all year into the nearby Sierra de San Francisco to see some of the 500 caves painted by the original inhabitants of the area centuries ago (but they can only be reached by 4WD or horse- or mule-back).

✚ 28A3

Museo Pinturas Rupestres
✉ Misión de San Ignacio
☎ (615) 154 0222
🕐 Mon–Fri 8–3
♿ Moderate

An oasis in the desert – the mission town of San Ignacio still has immense charm

Pacific Mexico

Mexico's oldest beach playgrounds are located along the Pacific coastline between Mazatlán and Acapulco. This is where the country's most dramatic beaches are found, backed by the craggy outline of the Sierra Madre del Sur. Glitzy favorites such as Acapulco and Puerto Vallarta are now joined by Ixtapa-Zihuatanejo, a burgeoning twin resort, and quieter destinations such as San Blas and Barra de Navidad, which offer a more genuine Mexican atmosphere. Long tracts of coastline remain undeveloped, while short forays can be made inland to hill villages where church bells are the only interruption to a peaceful existence. Watersports are king in these deep blue waters that are sometimes unsuitable for swimming due to their treacherous currents. Acapulco and Puerto Vallarta are the places to go for nightlife, good restaurants, and shopping.

> *"No American records survive,*
> *save in the vague traditions*
> *about 'white men' from the west,*
> *those mysterious 'snake peoples',*
> *regarding the voyages made*
> *across the Pacific to America by*
> *ancient Asian mariners".*

DONALD A MACKENZIE
Myths of Pre-Colombian America (c1910)

———————•———————

Local fishermen at the Pacific resort of Mazatlán

High-rises may line the bay but Acapulco is still a dramatic sight

Acapulco

A stunning sweep of bay heralded Acapulco's rise to fame in the 1950s, a revival of its 16th-century fortunes when it was developed by Cortés and his men as a port. In 1565 the first galleon set sail from Manila in the Philippines (then under Spanish rule) to Acapulco, marking the beginning of a flourishing trade route that saw the wealth of the Orient exchanged with that of Nueva España.

Craggy cliffs at the western end of the bay are the launch-pad for Acapulco's fearless divers

With an international airport and a fast toll road from Mexico City, Acapulco's fortunes are assured. Lining its 11km (7 mile) horseshoe bay are endless high-rise hotels, night-clubs, restaurants, and a string of beaches where watersports and sun-worshipping set the tone. A concrete jungle or a steamy, sybaritic holiday playground? Opinions are divided, but every visitor is at least won over by the stunning scenery.

From the eastern headland of Playa Bruja, the Costera Miguel Alemán sweeps past a succession of facilities that include five golf courses, children's recreation parks, a crafts market and the San Diego Fort high above the old town, before the bay twists into a peninsula. To the west is the towering cliff of La Quebrada, where daredevil divers plunge into the waves, and beyond this the tranquil beach and Coyuca Lagoon at Pie de la Cuesta. Air-conditioned buses shuttle along the front, making travel easy. Family holidays are much helped by this excellent infrastructure, but remember that Acapulco is an oasis in one of Mexico's poorest states.

What to See in Acapulco

FUERTE DE SAN DIEGO ✪✪
Overlooking the lively, narrow streets of the old town is this striking stone fort, with panoramic views over the bay and mountains. It was completed in 1617 to protect the thriving port from pirate and buccaneer attacks (including England's notorious Sir Francis Drake). Today, it functions as the Museo Histórico, with interesting historical and ethnographic exhibits.

72C1
Calle Morelos and Playa Hornitos
(744) 484 4583
Tue–Sun 10–6
Playa Los Hornos, Costera Miguel Alemán
(74) 844583

ISLA LA ROQUETA ✪
A few hundred yards off the Peninsula de las Playas, this small island, reached by glass-bottomed boats from below the Fuerte de San Diego, offers relaxing respite from the main Costera. Cross the island to reach a small, secluded bay with a restaurant, or climb to the lighthouse. The waters are targeted by scuba divers, who come to see the underwater shrine of La Virgen Sumergida.

72C1
Off Peninsula de las Playas

Tourist boats at the ready on Laguna Coyuca at Pie de la Cuesta

PIE DE LA CUESTA ✪✪
This long, narrow spit of land separating the Pacific from the mangrove and palm-fringed Laguna Coyuca is a favorite with waterskiers. Sunset fanatics home in on the beach to watch the painted sky from a beach bar hammock and sponsor daredevil locals to pit their strength against the thundering surf. Sadly, in 1997 Hurricane Pauline did extensive damage to this stretch and it will be some time before it regains its idyllic backdrop.

72C1
11km (7 miles) northwest of Acapulco

LA QUEBRADA ✪✪✪
Acapulco's high divers plunge over 40m (131ft) from this cliff into the crashing surf of a narrow cove below. This sight is even more spectacular after sundown, when the last divers carry lighted torches as they plunge. Have dinner or a drink while you witness this carefully timed feat of bravura.

72C1
Hotel Plaza Las Glorias, La Mira
Daily at 1, 7:30, 8:30, 9:30, 10:30PM
Good
Cheap

Freshly shucked oysters at one of Barra de Navidad's friendly beach restaurants

What to See in Pacific Mexico

BARRA DE NAVIDAD ✪

This picturesque fishing village developed only recently into an alternative beach resort to soulless Manzanillo, about 60km (37 miles) south. Built on a sandbar next to a large estuary, Barra town offers modest hotels and restaurants, and safe swimming in a scenic setting. Towering above the town is the relatively new resort Grand Bay Hotel, Isla Navidad, boasting a 27-hole golf course, a beach club with many watersports, and a glitzy marina.

🗓 72A2
✉ 60km (37 miles) north of Manzanillo
ℹ (315) 355 5100

IXTAPA-ZIHUATANEJO ✪✪

These twin resort towns are only 6km (4 miles) apart, yet have very different characters. Ixtapa is the modern half, its beachfront lined with high-rise hotels squeezed along the long white-sand Playa del Palmar. The wide bay dotted with tiny islands offers boat trips, windsurfing, waterskiing and diving, but swimming can be dangerous. When the waves are strong, head for Isla Ixtapa, where a secluded beach fronts a nature reserve. Ixtapa also offers excursions to lagoons, horse riding, sport fishing, golf, and diving.

For some, the former fishing-village setting of Zihuatanejo, with forested headlands plunging into secluded bays, is preferable. Although it is a jazzed-up version of its former self, it offers more atmosphere and older, less pretentious hotels. The least attractive beach, Playa Principal, edges the old town, but beyond a headland to the southeast are Playa Madera, a family beach with economical hotels; Playa la Ropa, home to chic hotels; and Playa Las Gatas, only accessible by boat. Other attractions are the scenic road winding high over the headland to Playa la Ropa, and a new walkway connecting the main town beach with Playa Madera.

🗓 72B1
🚤 Motorboats run all day from Playa Quieta, Ixtapa's northern beach, or sail there with Yates del Sol from Puerto Mio marina
🍴 Seafood restaurants ($)
ℹ Ixtapa shopping mall ☎ (755) 553 1967

A Walk in Puerto Vallarta

This walk winds through atmospheric cobbled streets and leads you across the Río Cuale (➤ 67) to where the Mexican heart still beats.

Start at the church on the main square of Old Vallarta.

The curious crown that tops Nuestra Señora de Guadalupe is a replica of the hapless Empress Carlota's crown. It fell off in a 1994 earthquake, but is now perfectly restored.

Leave the church, turn right into Hidalgo and right again up Iturbide. Climb two steep blocks to Carranza and turn right.

At the end of this street on the left is the Callejón de los Tarques, crossed by the bridge that Elizabeth Taylor and Richard Burton built to connect their two houses. There is a lovely view south from the corner.

Return along Carranza as far as Corona. Turn left and walk two blocks downhill for another superb view, looking north. Walk along Matamoros for five blocks, then turn left at Libertad. This goes over the Río Cuale into Insurgentes. Turn left at Lázaro Cárdenas.

On your left is Santa Cruz (built 1902), a popular neighborhood church.

Continue three blocks further to the Emiliano Zapata market on your right before turning left down Camichín. Climb a few steps at the end to a riverside road. Follow it into Áquiles Serdán and walk straight on, crossing Insurgentes, to Ignacio Vallarta, then turn right. This brings you to steps down on to the Isla Cuale below. Walk west towards the sea.

On your right is the small Museo del Cuale (➤ 66), with an interesting collection of pottery, sculptures and other artifacts from Jalisco, Narayit, and Colima.

The heart of Old Vallarta surrounds the unmistakable campanile of Nuestra Señora de Guadalupe

Distance
3km (2 miles)

Time
2 hours

Start point
Nuestra Señora de Guadalupe, Old Vallarta
➕ 72A2

End point
Isla Cuale
➕ 72A2

Lunch
Daiquri Dick's Restaurant/Bar ($–$$)
✉ Olas Altas 314
☎ (322) 222 0566

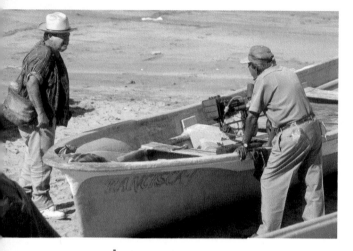

➕ 28B2
ℹ️ Edificio Banrural, Avenida
Camarón Sábalo, corner
Tiburón ☎ (669) 916
5160

Museo Arqueológico de Mazatlán

✉️ Sixto Osuna 76, Paseo
Olas Altas
☎ (669) 981 1455
🕐 Tue–Sun 10–3
🍴 Cafés ($) on Plazuela
Machado
♿ Few
💲 Cheap

Mexico's largest shrimp-fishing fleet is based at Mazatlán

➕ 72A2
ℹ️ Juarez y Independencia
☎ (322) 223 2500

Museo del Cuale

✉️ Isla Cuale
🕐 Tue–Sat 10–3, 4–7, Sun
10–2
🍴 Cafés and restaurants
($$) nearby
♿ None

MAZATLÁN ✪

This sprawling resort town is also the largest west coast port between Los Angeles and the Panama Canal, a factor that makes it less commercialized than Mexico's other resorts. Jutting out on a peninsula marked by three hills, its beaches stretch for about 8km (5 miles), lined by a sea-wall promenade, the *malecón*, which ends at the headland lighthouse of Olas Altas. Behind this hilltop lies the commercial port and old town, while to the far north, Mazatlán's Zona Hotelera monopolizes the seafront.

Despite the influx of tourism, initially attracted by rich sport fishing, Mazatlán still depends on its fishing industry, with tuna-canning factories and shrimp-freezing plants supplied daily by Mexico's largest shrimp fleet. Fish aside, it offers great sports (golf, tennis, riding, watersports), boat trips to two islands with pristine beaches and an atmospheric old town center with a gracious old theater, cathedral, and a small **archaeological museum**, which displays locally excavated artifacts.

PUERTO VALLARTA ✪✪✪

Ever expanding and ever popular, Puerto Vallarta is located on Mexico's largest bay, the Bahía de Banderas. It acquired international fame in 1964 when John Huston's film *The Night of the Iguana* hit the screens, with a hot background romance between Richard Burton and Elizabeth Taylor. At that time Vallarta was just a quaint little fishing village with cobbled streets and tile-roofed houses. Today this aspect still exists (▶ 65), as does a moody backdrop of thickly forested hills that sometimes plunge straight into the Pacific, but beyond are high-rise hotels and condos, a marina, hip nightclubs, cosmopolitan restaurants and a vast array of high-quality stores.

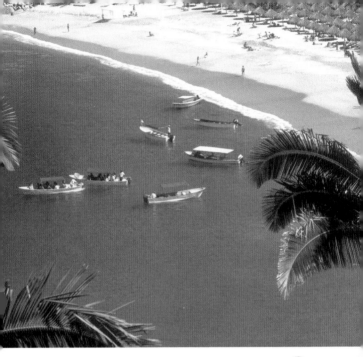

Developments are spreading fast at both ends of the bay, to Mismaloya in the south, where an underwater park lies around the outlying rocks of Los Arcos, and 18km (11 miles) north to the self-contained Nueva Vallarta. Boat trips spirit you to beauty spots such as Boca de Tomatlán, Yelapa, or the Islas Marietas, off Punta Mita. Equally scenic are the roads through the hills, such as to El Tuito; horseback riding or biking are a good alternative to jeeps.

Old Vallarta is still unsurpassed for atmosphere; don't miss the *malecón* and Río Cuale environs. An island at the mouth of this river is home to the **Museo del Cuale** (► 66), restaurants, and craft shops while on its north bank is the *malecón*, town hall and idiosyncratic church. The backstreets here are packed with intriguing stores and art galleries. The liveliest town beach, day and night, is Playa Los Muertos, at the southern end of the town center.

SAN BLAS ✪✪

If you have a good insect repellent and revel in sleepy, unspoilt seaside towns, then this is where to go. Surfing is the number-one activity here, closely followed by bird-watching in the mangrove-fringed estuaries and La Tovara lagoon. From November to March over 200 migrating species join the 150 native species. The bay was an important 16th- to 18th-century departure point for Spanish expeditions, and ruins from this period include the old Aduana (Custom's House), the hilltop Fuerte de Basilio, and a 1769 church.

✚ 72A3
✉ 130km (81 miles) NW of Puerto Vallarta
🛈 Palacio Municipal ☎ (323) 285 0005

Top: *Playa Mismaloya, location of* Night of the Iguana*; above: guardian angel of fishermen on Vallarta's* malecón

67

In the Know

If you only have a short time to visit Mexico, or would like to get a real flavor of the country, here are some ideas:

10
Ways to Be a Local

Squeeze lime on your food at every opportunity—allegedly, it kills bacteria.

When it's hot, spend the afternoon hours inside, in a shaded hammock or under a *palapa*.

Wear a hat: rancho-style in the north, Panama-style in the south.

Light a candle to the Virgen de Guadalupe.

Eat *tortillas* as if there is no tomorrow.

Be generous with *pesos* to street artists and adult beggars.

Take provisions with you on long bus trips: express buses do not always stop.

In Mexico City, after dark only use radio-taxis (*sitios*).

Haggle for local crafts at markets.

Be patient at every turn; the Mexican sense of time is very different, as you will learn.

10
Good Places to Have Lunch

Beto's Condesa ($$) ✉ Playa Condesa, Costera Miguel Aleman, Acapulco ☎ (744) 484 0100/0473. Popular beachfront restaurant where you have the tantalizing choice between lobster and succulent steaks.

Caesar's ($$) ✉ Emiliano Zapata, corner Benito Juárez, Loreto ☎ (613) 133 0203. Bustling seafood restaurant in center of Loreto: a must for anyone in the area.

Café del Bosque ($$) ✉ Off Paseo de la Reforma, Bosque de Chapultepec, Mexico City ☎ (55) 5515 4652/5516 4214. Lakeside restaurant in Chapultepec Park. Mexican and

international dishes with live *marimba* music.

Café la Gloria ($$) ✉ Vicente Suárez 41, corner Amatlan, Colonia Condesa, Mexico City ☎ (55) 5211 4180. In the arty, leafy quarter of Colonia Condesa. Informal, popular lunch spot with pavement tables serving international cuisine. Young, colorful clientele.

El Anclote ($–$$) ✉ Playa El Anclote, Punta Mita, Puerto Vallarta ☎ (322) 222 1949. Flee to the northernmost headland of Bahía de Banderas for the ultimate beachside lunch. Seafood soup, beef, chicken or fresh lobster.

El Tule ($$$) ✉ Hotel Victoria, Lomas del Fortin 1, Oaxaca ☎ (951) 515 2633. Panoramic hotel restaurant on the hillside. Regional specialties and international cuisine.

Gran Café del Portal ($) ✉ Independencia, corner Zamora, Veracruz ☎ (228) 932 9339. A Veracruz institution, founded in 1810 as La Parroquia. Breakfasts extend into lunches; much favored by local dignitaries.

La Casona ($$) ✉ Calle 60, No 434, Mérida ☎ (999) 923 8348. Beautifully restored mansion with attractive patio and garden for cool lunches. Italian cuisine.

Left: *resting in the desert sunshine*
Right: *horseback riding along a rough, steep track*

Los Pacos ($$)
✉ Constitución 104, Oaxaca ☎ (951) 516 1704. Uninhibited views of Santo Domingo from the top terrace which is open at lunch. Sophisticated Oaxacan dishes.

Restaurant Bella Italia ($)
✉ Hernandez Macias 50, San Miguel de Allende ☎ (415) 152 4989. Sunny garden courtyard for devouring delicious Italian dishes away from shopaholic crowds.

Observing underwater wonders with snorkel and mask

Top Activities

Horseback riding in Baja California's Sierra de la Giganta or in the hills around Oaxaca

Whale-watching (Dec–Apr) in Baja California

Rocking along in the Chihuahua–Pacifico Copper Canyon train

Watching the divers at La Quebrada, Acapulco

Parasailing at Acapulco, Ixtapa, Cancún or Puerto Vallarta

Hooking a marlin in the Mar de Cortés

Diving in the Caribbean at Los Manchones, off Isla Mujeres

Playing golf at the top 18-hole course designed by Jack Nicklaus at Cabo del Sol, Los Cabos

Kayaking across the Bahía de Banderas, off Puerto Vallarta

Swimming with dolphins on Isla Mujeres or on Cozumel

Top Handicraft Buys

- Handblown glass from Tonalá, Guadalajara
- Decorative tinwork from Oaxaca
- Silver jewelry and tableware from Taxco
- Handwoven textiles from Chiapas and Oaxaca
- Talavera ceramics from Puebla or cheaper look-alikes from Dolores Hidalgo

Best Baroque Churches

- Capilla del Rosario in Puebla's Santo Domingo
- Templo de la Valenciana in Guanajuato
- Santa Clara and Santa Rosa in Querétaro
- Santo Domingo in Oaxaca
- Santo Domingo in San Cristóbal

Best Fruits, Fresh or in Drinks

- *Guanabana*, soursop (related to the custard-apple)
- *Piña*, pineapple
- *Papaya*, pawpaw, eaten doused in lime juice

- *Mango*, but not the green variety used for preserves
- *Naranja*, orange, delicious in juices when mixed with *mandarina* (mandarin) or *zanahoria* (carrot)

Best Climbs

- Iztaccíhuatl, the sister volcano to Popocatépetl, for a close-up on Popo's rising steam
- The church of Nuestra Señora de Los Remedios, atop the largest pyramid in the Americas at Cholula
- The Pirámide de la Luna at Teotihuacán for a clear view of early town-planning
- Cheat at Taxco and take the cable-car up to Monte de Taxco
- The giant statue of Morelos on the island of Janitzio overlooking Lago de Pátzcuaro
- El Faro (the lighthouse) at Mazatlán, the world's second-highest natural lighthouse after Gibraltar
- The dunes at Faro Viejo in Cabo San Lucas, for panoramic ocean views
- Nohuch Mul at Cobá, the tallest pyramid on the northern Yucatán peninsula, for sweeping jungle views
- The Torre Latino-americana in Mexico City: another cheat as you'll be in a lift
- El Castillo, at the heart of Chichén Itzá

The South

Indigenous people account for over 75 percent of the population, adding a clear visual presence to this region. Beyond apparently deserted hills are villages with firmly entrenched customs and craft traditions. Hugging the coast to the north is the state of Veracruz, land of riotous February carnivals and *marimba* bands that impart a distinctly tropical, almost Caribbean atmosphere. Oaxaca, to the south, remains queen of history, archaeology, culture, and crafts. East of Veracruz is the oil-rich state of Tabasco, once the heart of Mesoamerica's oldest civilization, the Olmecs, but now clearly a front-runner in fast-developing Mexico. Furthest south is the troubled region of Chiapas, where indigenous people have suffered at the hands of landowners and economic interests for centuries. This, too, is where high, pine-clad mountains alternate with tropical rainforests that conceal evocative Mayan ruins.

> *"Luxuriant vegetation of emerald hue bends in flower-laden branches to the waters' edge, overarched by a sky of purest azure; brilliant-hued butterflies and humming-birds with metallic sheen fly from flower to flower…"*

TEOBERT MALER
Memoirs of the Peabody Museum (1908–10)

───────── ● ─────────

The interior of the Templo de Santo Domingo, jewel of Oaxaca

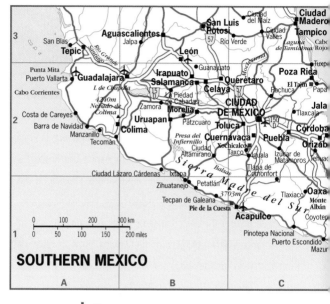

3

San Blas
Tepic

Punta Mita
Puerto Vallarta
Cabo Corrientes
Guadalajara
L de Chapala

4210m
Nevado de Colima

Costa de Careyes
Barra de Navidad
Manzanillo
Tecomán
Colima
Uruapan

Aguascalientes
Jalpa

León
Guanajuato

Irapuato
Salamanca
Celaya
La Piedad
de Cabadas
Zamora
Morelia
Pátzcuaro

Ciudad
del Maíz

San Luis
Potosí
57
Río Verde

Ciudad
Valles

Querétaro

CIUDAD
DE MÉXICO

Toluca
Cuernavaca
Presa del Infiernillo
Ciudad
Altamirano
Xochicalco
Taxco

Puebla

Ciudad
Madero
Tampico
Laguna de Tamiahua Cabo
Rojo
Tuxp
Poza Rica
El Tajín
Pachuca Papa

Jala
Tlaxcala

Córdoba
Orizab
Izúcar de
Matamoros Xehuac

Ciudad Lázaro Cárdenas
Ixtapa
Zihuatanejo
Petatlán

Iguala
Tlapa de
Comonfort

Sierra Madre

3703m

del Sur

Oaxa
Monte
Albán
Coyotep

Tecpan de Galeana
Pie de la Cuesta

Balsas

Tlaxiaco

2

1

Acapulco

Pinotepa Nacional
Puerto Escondido
Mazur

| 0 | 100 | 200 | 300 km |
| 0 | 50 | 100 | 150 | 200 miles |

SOUTHERN MEXICO

A   B   C

Oaxaca

**Oaxaca, capital of the state of the same name, is a
graceful, small-scale city where the sun seems to
shine permanently on the distant hills. Unique,
colorful and full of surprises, it is one of Mexico's
most relaxed, pleasurable towns. History is
omnipresent yet not overpowering, while markets,
art galleries, craft shops, cafés, and restaurants
make for endless tempting distractions.**

At Oaxaca's heart is a magnificent *zócalo* rimmed by cafés,
and a genuine crossroads for anyone in town—resident,
visitor, or shoeshiner alike. Once the center for the Mixtec
and Zapotec civilizations, Oaxaca rapidly developed a
strong Spanish flavor after it was conquered in 1533.
Countless churches (including the masterful baroque Santo
Domingo), elegant mansions, government buildings,
decorative grille-work, and charming plazas were built,
creating a harmonious backdrop for the strikingly proud
indigenous population.

In 1987 Oaxaca, together with Monte Albán, a fabulous
legacy of the Zapotecs (► 20) was declared a world

heritage site by UNESCO, and since then seems not to have looked back. Excellent services, atmospheric hotels, and a network of craft villages have all been organized and made accessible, offering a wide choice of activities to the visitor. The silhouette of the Sierra Madre del Sur is a constant reminder of its rural attractions, whether on horseback, bicycle, or by car. However Oaxaca's charm is best enjoyed through strolls through cobbled streets, past brightly painted houses brimming with flowers, peeping into churches or courtyards, checking out shops, or people-watching on the *zócalo*.

Benito Juárez market in Oaxaca

What to See in Oaxaca

MUSEO DE LAS CULTURAS DE OAXACA ✪✪✪

Next door to Santo Domingo is the former Dominican monastery that now houses the regional museum, backed by a newly landscaped botanical garden. The rooms and vaulted cloisters of this building display the wealth of archaeological artifacts found in the state. Pride of place goes to the fantastic collection of Mixtec jewelry found in Tomb 7 at Monte Albán, including gold, turquoise, rock-crystal, jade, and silver.

MUSEO RUFINO TAMAYO ✪✪

The late Rufino Tamayo, one of Mexico's foremost 20th-century painters and a native of Oaxaca, spent over 20 years collecting pre-Hispanic antiquities, and this small, select museum is the result. Five color-coordinated rooms display some exceptional pieces, in particular those devoted to the Olmec, Occidente, Totonac, and Maya cultures. Concerts and art exhibitions are also held here.

TEMPLO DE SANTO DOMINGO ✪✪

Started in the late 16th century, this church is one of Mexico's finest examples of baroque architecture. Above the main entrance is an extraordinary bas-relief genealogical tree of the family of Domingo de Guzmán, the 13th-century founder of the Dominican order. Beyond this, the soaring ceiling is entirely faced in elaborately gilded and painted stucco, surrounding 36 inset paintings. To the right is the Capilla del Rosario, another magnificent interpretation of Mexican baroque by indigenous artisans.

✚ 72C1
✉ Ex-Convento de Santo Domingo, Alcalá
☎ (951) 516 2991
🕐 Tue–Sun 10–8
ℹ García Vigil 517 and Reforma 526
♿ Good
🍴 Moderate; free Sun

✚ 72C1
✉ Morelos 503
☎ (951) 516 4750
🕐 Wed–Sat, Mon 10–2, 4–7, Sun 10–3
♿ Very good
🍴 Cheap

✚ 72C1
✉ Alcalá, corner Gurrión
🕐 Mon–Sat 8–7:30, Sun 7–11AM, 1–7:30PM
♿ Good
🍴 Free

Below: *an exhibit at Museo Rufino Tamayo*

Right: *the defensive style of the Templo de Santo Domingo was intended to deter attack*

74

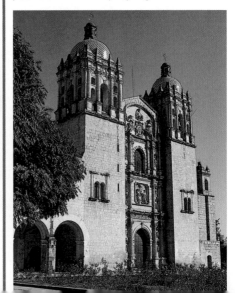

A Walk around Oaxaca

This walk through the colonial heart of Oaxaca takes in churches, museums, and the city's inimitable atmosphere.

Start at the zócalo and head for the Catedral on the north side.

Built in 1533, it contains a bronze altar, antique organ, and, best of all, an elaborate 18th-century baroque facade.

Leave the Catedral, turning sharp right, and walk along Independencia to the pedestrian street of Alcalá. Turn left and walk uphill to the Museo de Arte Contemporáneo. After visiting, continue uphill, turn right along Murguia as far as Cinco de Mayo, then turn left. On your right is the Camino Real Hotel.

This 400-year-old former convent of Santa Catalina, now a national monument, is very picturesque and exudes a distinctive atmosphere.

Continue uphill to Santo Domingo and visit both the church and adjacent museum. On leaving, turn right past the Instituto de Artes Gráficas to the Plazuela del Carmen Alto.

This small plaza is home to a colorful daily market of Oaxacan crafts.

Leave the plaza, turning left into García Vigil. Continue downhill for four blocks before turning right into Morelos. Two blocks further is the Museo Rufino Tamayo. After visiting, continue another two blocks.

On the left is the Basílica de la Soledad, a late-17th-century church, home to a statue of the town's patron saint and a small museum.

Walk down the steps to Independencia. Turn left and walk four blocks east to the church of San Felipe Neri.

This church (1636) is noted for its fine frescoed walls and ornately gilded altar and nave.

Continue along Independencia to the zócalo.

Distance
2km (1 mile)

Time
3 hours including stops

Start/end point
Zócalo
🚑 72C1

Lunch
Café del Instituto de Artes Gráficas ($)
✉ Alcalá 507
☎ (951) 516 2045

Oaxaca's treasure-trove of crafts is hard to bypass

A Drive in Oaxaca Valley

This drive covers the valley southeast of the state capital, taking in crafts villages and archaeological sites.

Leave Oaxaca by following signs to Istmo or Tehuantepec, which bring you to Highway 190. You soon enter the village of El Tule, with its colorful church and giant tree.

This gnarled *ahuehuete* tree is claimed to be the world's largest tree with a circumference of 58m; it is thought to be some 2,000 years old and is still sprouting.

Continue 6km on the highway to a turn-off on the right to Tlacochuaya.

The ridges and whorls of the venerable ahuehuete (cypress) tree in El Tule

Here a magnificent church stands within a Dominican monastery complex, its interior notable for ornate floral murals and a 16th-century organ.

Return to the highway, continue east, stopping at the archaeological site of Dainzú before turning left to Teotitlán del Valle, famed for its hand–woven rugs. Return and continue along the highway to another turn-off on the left to Yagul.

This little-visited Zapotec site sits high in the cacti-studded hills and offers fabulous 360-degree views of the valley. Its ball court is the second largest in Mesoamerica.

Follow the highway to an intersection, take the left fork to Mitla. Drive into the village plaza.

Visit the Frissell Museum before walking uphill past numerous crafts outlets to the red-domed church, crafts market and the superb Zapotec structures (► 77).

Continue east from Mitla to a turn-off to Hierve del Agua. An unsurfaced road leads to this sensational site—a petrified mineral waterfall and pools. Return to Oaxaca by the same route.

Distance
120km

Time
5–6 hours, depending on stops

Start/end point
Oaxaca
➕ 72C1

Lunch
Centeotl ($)
✉ Zona Arqueológica Yagul
☎ (951) 562 0289

What to See in the South

HUATULCO (► 19, TOP TEN)

MAZUNTE ✪

This delightful, low-key fishing village lies 62km (39 miles) west of Huatulco, between Puerto Angel and Puerto Escondido. A beautiful adjoining beach, San Agustinillo, is a favorite among Mexicans for long lunches under shady *palapas*. Outlying rocks shelter the beach, making it ideal for those in search of calm waters and fresh seafood. Mazunte itself is home to the world's only turtle research center and museum (**Museo de la Tortuga**), an impressive modern set-up with turtles representing 9 of the world's 11 types. The wild 15km (9 mile) beach north of here, not accessible by road, sees the arrival of some 200,000 Olive Ridley turtles during their nesting season, from July to December. Mazunte is also home to a local enterprise making natural cosmetics.

MITLA ✪✪

Meaning "place of the dead," this fascinating Zapotec site was occupied between AD 400 and 700 but then became solely a ceremonial center. Much of the rich stone-carving was finished by the later Mixtecs, who alternated with the Zapotecs in regional power until the Spanish arrived in 1521. The structures are famed for their complex geometrical stonework, made using an inlay technique. This is particularly well preserved in the Grupo de las Columnas, which contains the masterful Patio de las Grecas. Nearby, another patio structure incorporates two underground cruciform tombs.

The remains of Mixtec murals are displayed in the grounds of the red-domed 16th-century church that rises above the site. Behind it is a large crafts market. The village is dominated by small crafts shops and *mezcal* bars, but don't miss the Frissell Museum, on the plaza at the entrance.

MONTE ALBÁN (► 20, TOP TEN)

Zapotec stone inlay techniques created 14 different patterns on the palaces and tombs of Mitla

---

✚ 72C1

Museo de la Tortuga
- ✉ On main road (Mex 200)
- ☎ (958) 584 3055
- 🕐 Wed–Sat 10–4:30
- 🍴 Excellent seafood restaurants ($) in Playa San Agustinillo
- ♿ None
- 🎟 Cheap

✚ 73D1
- ✉ Highway 190, 45km (28 miles) from Oaxaca
- 🕐 Daily 8–5
- 🍴 Cafés and restaurants ($) in village
- ♿ Few
- 🎟 Cheap; free Sun

77

PALENQUE (▶ 22, TOP TEN)

PUERTO ÁNGEL   ✪✪

This charming fishing port, nestling between forested hills, has long been a favorite of those in the know. However, in 1997 Hurricane Pauline caused extensive damage, and although reconstruction was rapid, some scars still remain.

There is little to do here except lap up the sun, lazing on the pretty Playa Panteon and watching diving pelicans, but the slow pace is appealing and the locals are extremely friendly. Ultra-fresh seafood is provided by fishermen who beach their boats or moor at the jetty. A short distance northwest is the hippy beach of Zipolite, where thatched beach huts again suffered from the hurricane, but the white sands ending in rocky headlands still attract backpackers, while surfers revel in the often wild waves. Currents are dangerous and drownings have occurred.

PUERTO ESCONDIDO   ✪✪

Of the three beach resorts scattered along the Oaxacan coast, Puerto Escondido takes the middle road between sophisticated Huatulco (▶ 19) and relaxed Puerto Ángel. Its fishing-village past has receded somewhat with the influx of hotels, restaurants and shops, but the lovely curved bay is only the beginning; to the east lie palm-fringed Playa Marinero and the surfers' paradise of Playa Zicatela, while to the west is the pretty cove of Puerto Ángelito, accessible by boat or road. From Playa Principal a walkway winds around the cliffs, offering sweeping sea views. Nightlife thrives in the form of low-key beach bars.

✚ 73D1

✉ 83km (52 miles) southeast of Puerto Escondido

🍴 Restaurant Susy ($), Playa del Panteon

The relaxed fishing village of Puerto Ángel

✚ 72C1

✉ 264km (164 miles) south of Oaxaca

ℹ Boulevard Benito Juárez s/n, Fraccionamento Bacocho ☎ (954) 582 0175

SAN CRISTOBAL DE LAS CASAS ★★★

This beautiful but politically troubled town, high in the forested hills east of Tuxtla, remains a prime tourist favorite. Wood smoke fills the air in the narrow cobbled streets, shops offer an amazing array of local crafts, and hotels and restaurants are reasonable. Unfortunately, since the Zapatistas' uprising of 1994 events have proved that little is being done to improve rural conditions, an ongoing problem for centuries.

The main sights in town are the restored cathedral on the main square and, uphill on Avenida General Utrilla, the fabulous church of Santo Domingo (1547). Transformed in the 18th century, it presents a lacy, carved facade and an ornate baroque interior. Its terraces throng with an impromptu crafts market daily, while the adjoining monastery houses the **Museo Regional** and the fascinating weavers' co-operative, **Sna Jolobil**. The latter displays and sells examples of the skilled techniques still practised by local communities. Handicrafts continue two blocks north at the labyrinthine Mercado. East of here is Na-Bolom, a fascinating institution founded by Frans Blom and his wife Trudy. They both extensively researched and supported local communities, leaving this house as a legacy to anthropologists and writers, who stay here.

San Cristóbal is also the starting point for excursions to local villages. San Juan Chamula, 9km (6 miles) north, has a large Sunday market in front of its extraordinary church. Here the Tzotzils carry on a form of worship that combines Christianity with ancient Mayan spiritual practices. Entry to the church is not allowed during religious ceremonies.

🔢 73E1

ℹ️ Delegacion de Turismo, Avenida Miguel Hidalgo 2
☎ (967) 678 6570/678 1467

Museo Regional

✉️ Ex-Convento de Santo Domingo
☎ (967) 81609
🕐 Daily 10–5
🚻 None
🍴 Cheap; free Sun

Sna Jolobil

✉️ Ex-Convento de Santo Domingo
☎ (967) 678 2646
🕐 Daily 10–5
🚻 None
🍴 Free

San Cristobal's Dominican church combines vast scale with ornately carved vegetal motifs

🗺 73E1
ℹ Belisario Domínguez 950
 ☎ (961) 612 5511

Museo Regional
✉ Parque Madero
☎ (961) 613 4479
🕐 Tue–Sun 9–4
🍴 Cafés ($) in park
♿ Good
💲 Cheap; free Sun

*The vertiginous depths of
the Cañon de Sumidero*

> ### Did you know ?
>
> *The indigenous people of Oaxaca and Chiapas have a
> rich tradition of weaving that varies greatly in pattern
> and color from village to village. Back-strap looms
> are used to create fabulous huipiles (tunics), the most
> exuberant being those of the Tzotzil and Tzetzil
> communities, decorated with pom-poms,
> tassels and satin ribbons.*

TUXTLA GUTIÉRREZ ★

Although not an essential attraction in itself, Tuxtla is at the crossroads of several outstanding southern destinations. This modern capital of the state of Chiapas lies in a hot saucer rimmed by hills that rise in the east to San Cristóbal de las Casas. In the town center is the Parque Madero, a cultural complex containing a theater, botanic gardens, and the **Museo Regional**, which has a good display of Olmec and Mayan artifacts. To the south is a unique and enlightened zoo (➤ 111).

Seventeen kilometers (10 miles) east, on Highway 190, is Chiapa de Corzo, Chiapas' first Spanish settlement, dating from 1528. The arcaded main square encloses a fountain structure, La Pila, built to resemble the Spanish crown. One block away is the vast church of Santo Domingo, whose former convent houses the Museo de la Laca (lacquer museum), a local craft specialty. Just behind flows the Río Grijalva. From the *embarcadero* (jetty) boats leave for tours of the Cañon de Sumidero. This canyon, with depths of over 1,000m (3,280ft), can also be viewed from lookout points along a road north of Tuxtla.

VERACRUZ ⭐⭐

Known above all for its riotous Shrovetide carnival, Veracruz was also the place where Hernán Cortés and his men first landed in 1519. This major port on the Gulf of Mexico later witnessed the arrival of French forces in 1838, and in 1847 was bombarded by the Americans. As a result, many of its monuments date from the late 19th century, with the exception of the beautiful **Fortaleza de San Juan de Ulua**, built in the 16th century and later much extended. Lying north of town in the main port area, the fort's sturdy walls and bastions, which once enclosed a political prison and presidential palace, now contain a museum.

Life in central Veracruz revolves around the Plaza de Armas, flanked by the Catedral (1734) and the fine Palacio Municipal (1627), where hawkers vie with *marimba* bands long into the steamy night. The aquarium (➤ 111) is also exceptional, but for swimming head south to the popular, though dirty, Mocambo beach, near Boca del Río.

➕ 73D2

Fortaleza de San Juan de Ulua
✉ Islote de San Juan de Ulúa
☎ (228) 938 5151
🕐 Tue–Sun 9–5
🍴 Drinks available
♿ Few
💷 Expensive

VILLAHERMOSA ⭐

The modern, oil-rich city of Villahermosa is famed, above all, for its relics of the sophisticated Olmec civilization, Mesoamerica's oldest. A large leisure complex, the Centro de Investigaciones de las Culturas Olmecas (CICOM), includes exceptional Olmec pieces at its Museo de Antropología, but it is at the **Parque Nacional de La Venta** that you will see the impressive giant heads that were hauled here from their original site at La Venta, 95km (59 miles) away. These now sit in a lush, wooded area that also houses an excellent zoo of local Tabasco animals. More insights into local nature lie at Yumka, a well-organized 100-hectare (247-acre) jungle, savannah and lagoon refuge for many endangered species (➤ 111).

➕ 73E2
ℹ Avenue Los Rios y Calle 13 Tabasio 2000, 86035 Villahermosa ☎ (993) 316 3633/316 2889

Parque Nacional de La Venta
✉ Boulevard Adolfo Ruiz Cortines
☎ (933) 314 1652
🕐 Tue–Sat 9–4:30
🍴 Cafeteria (£)
♿ Good
💷 Cheap; free Sun

An Olmec bas-relief at the open-air Parque Nacional de La Venta, just outside Villahermosa

The Yucatán Peninsula

Jutting out between the Gulf of Mexico and the Caribbean is a flat limestone shelf riddled with underground rivers, caves and *cenotes* (sinkholes). Above ground this peninsula is less than inspiring, consisting mainly of monotonous savannah and low jungle. Yet it continues to attract charter-loads of visitors. The reason is quite simple, this was the heartland of the great Maya culture and, along with Guatemala, claims their most astonishing monuments. Chichén Itzá, Uxmal, Cobá, and Tulum, as well as countless lesser-known sites, are a magnet for the historically inclined visitor. And beyond them lie the aquamarine depths of the Caribbean, where underwater life is hard to surpass. Lining the coast is a string of resorts, starting with Cancún, that cater for every touristic and hedonistic whim.

> **"***saw unexpectedly a spectacle of extraordinary beauty ... a large cavern or grotto, with a roof of broken, overhanging rock, high enough to give an air of wilderness and grandeur.* **"**

JOHN LLOYD STEPHENS
Incidents of Travel in the Yucatan
(1841)

———————•———————

Stone motifs of sky serpent masks adorn the facade of Uxmal's Cuadrángulo de las Monjas (the Nunnery)

✚ 73F2
ℹ Teatro Peón Contreras
☎ (999) 924 9290

Mérida

The elegant capital of the state of Yucatán makes a relaxed base for exploring major Mayan ruins such as Chichén Itzá (► 17) and Uxmal (► 89). Mérida has a strong sense of history and culture, much of which has been absorbed from its links with the U.S., Cuba, Europe, and even the Middle East. This unusually cosmopolitan flavor expanded further in the 1950s when direct road and rail links were established with Mexico City.

Despite enormous hardship, the Maya still find time to smile

When the Spaniards arrived in 1542, led by Francisco de Montejo, they used the stones of the declining Mayan city of T'ho to erect their cathedral and administrative structures. But it was not until the late 19th century that Mérida's fortunes really changed. The catalyst was the burgeoning sisal industry, whose prosperous French investors bequeathed an impressive *belle époque* architectural style. Today, many of the earlier colonial buildings around the *zócalo* have been restored, while to the north the tree-lined Paseo de Montejo is home to a string of grandiose edifices that were the residences of the sisal-empire builders. This area is now regarded as "modern" Mérida, targeted by airline offices, large hotels, and nightclubs.

South of the *zócalo*, in the streets surrounding the sprawling market, is a more mundane but authentic quarter, where everywhere you will see diminutive Mayan women in embroidered white dresses and older gentlemen in their immaculate white *guayaberas* (tucked shirts).

What to See in Mérida

CASA DE MONTEJO ✪✪

This is Mérida's first Spanish house, built in 1549 by the conquistador Francisco de Montejo. His descendants lived there until only a few years ago, but today the mansion more prosaically houses a branch of Banamex. The facade remains an outstanding example of the Plateresque style, with sculpted busts and the Montejo coat of arms depicting two soldiers triumphing over the bodies of prostrate Maya.

CATEDRAL DE SAN ILDEFONSO ✪✪

Built between 1556 and 1599, this is said to be the oldest cathedral on the American continent, although Campeche's inhabitants would not agree. The massive edifice was built with the stones of the dismantled Mayan town of T'ho, but during the 1915 Revolution it was stripped bare. Today's worshippers venerate an impressive 7m-tall statue of Christ that dominates the lofty stone interior. Other sights flanking the main square outside are the Palacio Municipal (1735) opposite, and the Palacio de Gobierno (1892) on the northern side, whose interior displays a remarkable series of 27 paintings depicting the complex history of the Maya, Spaniards, and Mexicans.

MUSEO DE ANTROPOLOGÍA E HISTORIA ✪✪

Located on Mérida's most salubrious avenue, this elaborate 1911 mansion was built for the state governor to rival others belonging to prosperous sisal barons. As a result, the interior Doric columns, marble, chandeliers, and extravagant mouldings somewhat overpower the exhibits. These offer a clear background to the history of the Yucatán, its Mayan sites, and culture. Artifacts include a rare collection of jade offerings recovered from the *cenote* at Chichén Itzá.

Mérida's elegant Casa de Montejo

🕂 73F2
✉ Plaza Mayor, Calle 63
🕐 Mon–Fri 9–5
🍴 Cafés and restaurants ($–$$) on square
🖐 Free

🕂 73F2
✉ Plaza Mayor, Calle 60
🕐 Daily 6AM–7PM
🍴 Cafés and restaurants ($–$$) on square and along Calle 60
♿ Few
🖐 Free

🕂 73F2
✉ Palacio Canton, Paseo de Montejo 485
☎ (999) 923 0557
🕐 Tue–Sat 8–8, Sun 8–2
🍴 Cafés and restaurants ($–$$) along Paseo de Montejo
♿ Few
🖐 Moderate; free Sun

8

Campeche's impressive fortified walls were built to repel pirates

What to See in the Yucatán Peninsula

CAMPECHE

Founded in the 1540s, Campeche suffered repeated attacks from pirates, and it was not until the erection of thick walls, reinforced by eight bastions, in the late 17th century that it prospered. There are two excellent museums and several interesting churches, including the Catedral on the main square and the 16th-century church of San Francisco. In the central Baluarte de la Soledad is a superb display of Mayan stelae, while to the south, in a **museum** in the hilltop Fuerte de San Miguel, is a rare collection of Mayan jade and pottery.

CANCÚN

Chosen by computer as the site of Mexico's largest resort in the early 1970s, Cancún attracts over 2.5 million visitors annually to indulge in powdery white-sand beaches, high-rise hotels, endless entertainment, sports and shopping. This is hardly the "real" Mexico, but makes an easy base for heading inland or further south along the increasingly developed "Maya Riviera." Most visitors come on package holidays and their 24-hour needs are well catered for. But long before the tourists came, there was a small Mayan settlement here, its remains are visible at the Ruinas del Rey and at the **Museo Arqueológico**.

CHICHÉN ITZÁ (► 17, TOP TEN)

COBÁ

This lakeside Mayan site remains little visited, despite its significance in the web of *sacbeob* (sacred "white paths") connecting other historic sites. Only a tiny proportion of this enormous city has been excavated, and these ruins are scattered through the jungle, so bring sturdy shoes, water, and insect repellent. Immediately visible is the Grupo de Cobá, whose narrow, steep pyramid rises over

Campeche
🕂 73E2
ℹ️ Calle 12 No 153, between Calle 55 and 53, also next to Catedral

Museo Histórico Fuerte de San Miguel
✉️ 4km (2.5 miles) south of Campeche
🕐 Tue–Sun 8–8
♿ Good
💵 Cheap

Cancún
🕂 73F3
ℹ️ Dirección de Turismo, Ayuntamiento, Avenida Tulum 5 ☎ (998) 887 4329

Museo Arqueológico
✉️ Centro de Convenciones, Km 9, Boulevard Kukulcán
☎ (998) 883 6671
🕐 Tue–Sun 8–7
🍴 Cafés and restaurants ($–$$) nearby
♿ Good
💵 Moderate; free Sun

Cobá
🕂 73F2
✉️ 42km (26 miles) northwest of Tulum
☎ (98) 324634
🕐 Daily 7AM–6PM
🍴 Cafés and restaurants ($)
💵 Moderate; free Sun

30m (98ft) above the tree-tops to give sweeping views over the lake. A ball court is next on the trail, followed by the Conjunto de las Pinturas (Temple of the Painted Ladies), some carved stelae and altars known as the Grupo Macanxoc. Nearly 3km (2 miles) further on towers 42m-high (138ft) Nohoch Mul, the tallest pyramid in the northern Yucatán peninsula. A strenuous climb is rewarded by a small temple decorated with descending god figures.

COZUMEL ✪

Like Cancún, the island of Cozumel is almost entirely geared to the needs of tourists. Cruise ship passengers, scuba divers and Cancunites all come to taste the delights of the renowned Palankar Reef, one of the world's top diving destinations. Unfortunately the most visited beach, Chankanab, now offers mainly dead coral, although the fish are spectacular. Skilled divers make day trips to some 20 different sites further out. Good swimming beaches dot the southwestern corner of the island, but strong currents make the eastern coast dangerous. In the unspoilt north lies a late Mayan site, **San Gervasio**. The main town, San Miguel, is a modernized place, where, again, the flavor of real Mexico is virtually absent.

+ 73F2
i Plaza del Sol, in the zocalo ☎ (987) 872 7563

San Gervasio
⊠ 13km (8 miles) northeast of San Miguel
☎ (987) 800 2215
◷ Daily 9–6
⛴ Frequent ferries from Playa del Carmen, boat trips from Cancún

Spectacular coral and shoals of brilliantly colored fish have put Cozumel firmly on the diver's map

GRUTAS DE LOLTÚN ✪✪

These spectacular underground caves and galleries lie in the heart of the undulating Puuc Hills, south of Mérida. Inhabited over 2,500 years ago, their secret network was also used by rebellious Maya seeking refuge during the mid-19th-century Caste War. Fabulous rock formations, cave paintings, musical stalactites and the Cathedral, a large chamber that soars over 50m (164ft) high, are all part of this compelling underworld.

+ 73E2
⊠ 115km (71 miles) south of Mérida, 50km (31 miles) east of Uxmal
◷ Daily guided tours at 9:30, 11, 12:30, 2, 3:30
🍽 Café ($) at entrance
♿ None
🎟 Moderate

🕇 73F3
ℹ Rueda Medina, opposite
jetty ☎ (998) 877 0307

Parque Nacional El Garrafón
✉ Carretera al Faro
☎ (998) 877 0318
🕐 Daily 9–4
🍴 Snack bar ($) on breezy
terrace
♿ None
💵 Moderate; free Sun

ISLA MUJERES

This delightful little island has a sleepy rhythm of its own. Most streets are of sand, cars are outnumbered by golf-carts and bicycles, and nights are tranquil. It makes an enticing escape from the over-development on Cancún, and as well as good beaches and diving, offers several attractions. The main town and services adjoin Playa Norte, while at the far southern tip is **El Garrafón**, a national park covering part of the Great Mayan Reef. Although the coral is dead, boat trips take snorkelers and divers to better spots further afield.

Half-way down the central lagoon lies Dolphin Discovery, a registered dolphin center, near a turtle farm. A small altar to the fertility goddess Ixchel explains the island's name (island of women); when the Spanish first landed they found numerous crude statues of her. Day trips also go to Isla Contoy, an uninhabited bird sanctuary.

🕇 73F3
☎ Free info-line 1-800-GO-
PLAYA

*Rocky cliffs slope down
to the sea at the southern
tip of Isla Mujeres*

PLAYA DEL CARMEN

Once a beach-bum's paradise, this small resort is mushrooming fast. The modern town center is built on a narrow grid of streets bisected by Avenida 5, a favorite promenading and restaurant strip, ending at palm-fringed Caribbean beaches. South of the Cozumel ferry pier is an airstrip and golf course, while north of town hotels are rapidly eating up the shore. Nightlife, eating, and shopping opportunities are plentiful, but there is little else.

🕇 73F2
✉ Highway 307
🕐 Daily 8–6
🍴 Snack bars ($) in plaza
♿ Few
💵 Moderate; free Sun

TULUM ●●

This dramatically sited Mayan ruin (AD 900–1500) rises perilously on a cliff edge north of a slowly expanding stretch of hotels. Inland lies a typical services town without much beauty but with reasonable prices. However, if you want a few quiet days sleeping beside the waves, Tulum's beach accommodation is ideal.

The ruins themselves are now fronted by a large

shopping plaza from where a tram ferries visitors to the site, although it is within easy walking distance. Sadly, this new structure has taken away much of Tulum's drama, but the Templo de los Frescos is still remarkable for its faded interior murals, the palace for its carved figures, and the Castillo complex for its serpentine columns and sweeping sea views.

UXMAL

😀😀😀

Uxmal was founded between the 5th and 6th centuries AD and at one point had some 25,000 inhabitants, before being abandoned around 900. It stands on a wide plateau in the Puuc Hills, near several smaller sites of similar style. Outstanding is the Pirámide del Adivino (Magician's Pyramid), an elliptical structure rising over 40m high. Immediately to the west stands the Cuadrángulo de las Monjas (The Nuns' Quadrangle), where fine stone inlay typifies the Puuc style. South of here is an elevated complex, the Palacio del Gobernador (Governor's Palace) showing unsurpassed decorative techniques. Beyond is the Casa de las Tortugas (House of the Turtles), the Gran Pirámide (Great Pyramid), and the Casa de la Vieja (Old Lady's House). Visitors with guides can see the last two structures where numerous sculpted phalluses at the Templo de los Falos (Temple of Phalluses) point to a unique cult in Uxmal.

Stone motifs on Uxmal's Cuadrángulo de las Monjas depict schematic Mayan huts and sky serpents

🗺 73E2
✉ 78km (48 miles) south of Mérida on Highway 261
🕐 Daily 8–5
🍴 Restaurant ($) in museum complex
♿ Few
💰 Moderate; free Sun
❓ Spectacular sound-and-light show at 7PM in Spanish, 9PM in English

Did you know ?

The sophisticated Mayan culture rose to prominence in the first centuries AD with the building of Palenque and other major sites in Guatemala, Belize, and Honduras. Between AD 600 and 900 Chichén Itzá, Uxmal, and Cobá reached their zenith, before being mysteriously abandoned. Over-population? Internal warfare? Drought? Hypotheses abound.

A Drive from Cancún to Cobá

Distance
350km (217 miles)

Time
9–10 hours (including stops)

Start/end point
Avenida López Portillo,
Cancún
✚ 73F3

Lunch
Hotel María de la Luz ($)
✉ Plaza Principal, Valladolid
☎ (985) 856 2071

This drive takes you inland from Cancún to the colonial town of Valladolid and the Mayan site of Cobá. A dip in a *cenote* is an option (➤ 114).

Drive west out of Cancún along Avenida López Portillo following signs for Valladolid/Mérida. Avoid the cuota highway (a pricey tollroad, though quicker) and remain on the old Highway 180 which takes you through a string of pretty rural villages.

Traditional Mayan houses are generally elliptical in shape with tightly aligned tree-branch walls and *palapa* (thatched palm-leaf) roofs.

Drive 159km (99 miles) to Valladolid, watching out for the countless topes (speed-breakers) that pepper every village. Drive straight into Valladolid's main plaza then follow Calle 41 west for two blocks, where it forks. Go left (Calle 41a) for another three blocks.

In front of you stands the bright yellow San Bernardino de Siena, a 16th-century Franciscan church and monastery. Often targeted by indigenous rebellions, the interior is practically bare.

Nohoch Mul, the tallest pyramid in the northern Yucatán peninsula

Continue southwest a few blocks to the Cenote Dzitnup, signposted on the outskirts.

Have a refreshing dip in this beautiful *cenote* before returning to the main plaza. Park, visit the church of San Servacio, shop, then have lunch.

Drive back 28km (17 miles) along Highway 180 to Chemax and turn right to Cobá. Another 30km (19 miles) brings you to this archaeological site (➤ 86). Leave Cobá by following signs to Tulum, then watch for a turn-off to the left after a few kilometers/miles. This brings you to Tres Reyes and back to Highway 180 or the toll road to Cancún.

Where To...

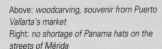

Above: *woodcarving, souvenir from Puerto Vallarta's market*
Right: *no shortage of Panama hats on the streets of Mérida*

91

Central Mexico

Price Categories

Restaurants are categorized as follows per person, including a beer or aperitif:

$ = up to $100 (pesos)
$$ = $100–150 (pesos)
$$$ = $150–250 (pesos)

Chiles en Nogada

This traditional Pueblan dish was once only available during the autumn pomegranate season, but deep-freezes have changed this. It consists of a gloriously creamy sauce of ground almonds and milk sprinkled with pomegranate seeds, coating a stuffed green pepper. At the heart of the dish is a complex stuffing of minced beef and veal, raisins, almonds and pine-nuts, all bound with egg. When it's good, it's very, very good!

Mexico City

Auseba ($$)

The Zona Rosa's traditional favorite for people-watching with tea or coffee and delicious cakes—try the *mousse au chocolat*.

✉ Hamburgo 159B, Zona Rosa
☎ (55) 5511 3770 🕐 Daily, 9AM–10:30PM, Sun from 11AM
🚇 Insurgentes

Bar l'Opéra ($$)

Sumptuously ornate *belle époque* decoration in this Parisian look-alike watering-hole. A favorite with artists and literati for evening drinks, but the food is mediocre.

✉ 5 de Mayo 10, Centro
☎ (55) 5512 8959 🕐 Daily 7PM–1AM 🚇 Bellas Artes

Café del Palacio ($$)

Choose between a sunny terrace overlooking Alameda Park or a superb art deco interior. The short but varied menu includes large, hygienically prepared salads and international dishes.

✉ Palacio de Bellas Artes, Avenida Juárez, Centro ☎ (55) 5512 3633 🕐 Tue–Sun 10–8, until 1AM after performances
🚇 Bellas Artes

Caffè Milano ($$)

An established Zona Rosa favorite for authentic Italian cuisine: pasta, fish and meat dishes. Outdoor tables or coolly designed interior.

✉ Amberes 27 ☎ (55) 5207 0119 🕐 Daily 8AM–2AM
🚇 Insurgentes

Cicero ($$$)

Refined Mexican cuisine in a theatrical hacienda-style setting, with antiques and a cosy wood-paneled bar. This is the place to indulge to the full—try the plantains stuffed with ground beef as a starter. Live music means a cover charge.

✉ Londres 195, Zona Rosa
☎ (55) 5512 6868 🕐 Mon–Sat 1PM–1AM 🚇 Sevilla

Los Girasoles ($$)

Elegant setting overlooking Plaza Tolsa. Exquisite Mexican *nouvelle cuisine* inspired by pre-Hispanic recipes and ingredients. Try the chicken in tamarind *mole*. Good service, innovative *mariachis*, bar.

✉ Tacuba 8/10, Centro
☎ (55) 5510 0630 🕐 Mon–Sat 1PM–1AM, Sun 1–6PM 🚇 Bellas Artes

Hostería de Santo Domingo ($)

Claims to be Mexico City's oldest restaurant. Graffiti liberally adorns the walls between old photos and pictures. The speciality is *chiles en nogada* all year round. Reasonable quality, erratic but friendly service.

✉ Belisario Domínguez 72, Centro ☎ (55) 5526 5276 🕐 Daily 10AM–10:30PM 🚇 Allende

Madero ($)

Popular local restaurant buzzing with afternoon activity. Good-value set menus served 2–5PM. Useful stop-over location between *Zócalo* and Bellas Artes.

✉ Francisco Madero 36, Centro ☎ (55) 5510 2761 🕐 Lunch, dinner daily until 9:30 🚇 Allende

San Angel Inn ($$$)

The place to lunch or dine in elegant San Angel. A superb 18th-century hacienda with gardens and patio. Award-winning international cuisine.

Booking essential, but the patio also functions as a relaxing bar.

✉ **Diego Rivera 50, corner Altavista, San Angel** ☎ **(55) 5616 0537** ⏱ **Mon–Sat 1PM–1AM, Sun 1–10PM**

Sanborns ($)

Spectacular atrium restaurant in the historic Casa de los Azulejos (House of Tiles). Digest afterwards looking at Orozco's 1925 mural, "Omniscience" or shop in the same establishment.

✉ **Francisco Madero 4, Centro** ☎ **(55) 5512 2300** ⏱ **Daily 7AM–1AM** 🚇 **San Juan de Letrán**

Guadalajara

El Abajeño ($$)

A Guadalajaran landmark with top *mariachis* thrown in. Attractive courtyard dining and bar, Jaliscan specialties, friendly service.

✉ **Avenida Vallarta 2802, Minerva** ☎ **(33) 363 0307** ⏱ **Lunch and dinner**

La Destilería ($$)

Combined restaurant and tequila museum with unmistakably Mexican décor and menu. Over 80 varieties of tequila (which originated in this state) are on offer.

✉ **Avenida México 2916** ☎ **(33) 3640 3110** ⏱ **Mon–Sat 1PM–midnight, Sun 1–6PM**

Guanajuato

Real de la Esperanza ($$)

Converted chapel set high above the town offering sweeping views, an outdoor bar area and sophisticated cuisine.

✉ **Carretera Guanajuato-Dolores Hidalgo Km 5, Valenciana** ☎ **(473) 732 1041** ⏱ **From 1PM**

Tasca de los Santos ($)

In a great location opposite the Basílica to catch the morning sun. Come here for the large breakfasts; paella is the specialty for later.

✉ **Plaza de la Paz 28** ☎ **(473) 732 2320** ⏱ **Daily 9AM–1AM**

El Truco ($)

An atmospheric, arty café/bar/ restaurant tucked down a side-street beside the Basílica. Good-value set menus. Lively background music.

✉ **Calle del Truco 7** ☎ **(473) 732 8374** ⏱ **Daily 9AM–midnight**

Querétaro

El Meson de Chico El Rota ($)

One of several terrace restaurants on the main square. Excellent Caesar salad and *nopalitos con queso*. Meat and seafood dishes.

✉ **Pasteur Sur 16, Centro** ☎ **(442) 212 4295** ⏱ **Daily for breakfast, lunch, dinner**

Meson de Santa Rosa ($$)

Stunning 300-year-old mansion-style hotel with romantic courtyard dining. Not to be missed, if only for a drink. Excellent, friendly service.

✉ **Pasteur 17 Sur** ☎ **(442) 242 2623** ⏱ **Lunch and dinner**

San Miguel del Allende

Restaurante Bella Italia ($)

Top-notch Italian cuisine. Freshly made pasta and salads in courtyard garden beside Bellas Artes. Good service and excellent value for money.

✉ **Hernández Macías 50** ☎ **(415) 152 4989** ⏱ **Lunch, dinner**

Mole

This is not some form of Mexican donkey but one of the country's most popular sauces used on chicken or turkey. Although the name is Náhuatl (the language of the Aztecs), legend has it that it was invented in a Pueblan convent by a group of nuns desperate to disguise the flavor of a rather scrawny turkey for the visit of a Viceroy. Into a basic chocolate sauce went numerous spices, herbs, chillies, cinnamon and almonds, which was then simmered slowly for three days. Today, although the *mole* specialists are the towns of Puebla and Oaxaca, the dish is widely available throughout the country and the sauce can be bought in the markets.

The North & Baja California

Cocktails and Margaritas

The term 'cocktail' is said to have originated in Mexico when British naval crews stopping in Campeche started mixing their rum with other ingredients. When mixing spoons ran out one day, an ingenious waiter introduced the root of a plant known as the "tail of a cock." By the 1920s cocktails, had become the rage in Europe and the U.S.A. Queen of this menu is the margarita, said to have originated in Chihuahua. The ingredients are white tequila, Triple Sec (or Cointreau), limes, crushed ice, and salt. In coastal resorts this is often served frozen.

Los Cabos

Da Giorgio ($$-$$$)

Acclaimed Italian restaurant in spectacular clifftop site. Home-made pasta, scampi, pizzas, seafood. Live music during season. New branch opened at Misiones del Cabo, overlooking El Arco.

✉ **Highway 1, San José del Cabo** ☎ **(624) 144 5304** ⏱ 1–11PM

Damiana ($$)

Colorful, romantic restaurant with patio dining at the heart of San José. Sophisticated cuisine includes char-broiled lobster and jumbo prawns.

✉ **Paseo Mijares 8, San José del Cabo** ☎ **(624) 142 0499** ⏱ **Daily 10:30AM–10:30PM** ❓ **Reservation recommended**

Mama Mia ($)

Popular, relaxed restaurant. International dishes, seafood, live music, fun atmosphere.

✉ **Km 29.5 Carretera Transpeninsular, San José del Cabo** ☎ **(624) 142 3940** ⏱ **Breakfast, lunch, and dinner**

Panchos ($)

Colorful Mexican restaurant offering hearty traditional dishes and seafood. Tortilla soup, *chile relleno* and lobster specialties. Live music nightly.

✉ **Calle Hidalgo, corner Zapata, Cabo San Lucas** ☎ **(624) 143 0973** ⏱ 6AM–11PM

Chihuahua

Chihuahua Charlie's ($)

A popular branch of the Anderson's chain of restaurants serving a wide choice of meat dishes and salads. Cheerful service and setting.

✉ **Avenida Juárez 3329** ☎ **(614) 415 7065**

Ensenada

El Rey Sol ($$$)

Award-winning restaurant serving French Provençal and Mexican dishes. Elegant, colonial-style setting.

✉ **Avenida López Mateos 1000** ☎ **(646) 178 1733** ⏱ **Lunch and dinner**

Guerrero Negro

Malarrimo ($–$$)

Delicious seafood including abalone, shrimp, and fish. Ask here about natural history and cave-painting tours.

✉ **Boulevard Emiliano Zapata (near entrance to town)** ☎ **(615) 157 0250**

Loreto

Café Olé ($)

Popular U.S.-style restaurant. Steaks, salads, and seafood; cheerful atmosphere.

✉ **Madero** ☎ **(613) 135 0496**

Cesar's ($$)

Acclaimed seafood in a well-established restaurant. Large portions of red snapper, lobster and other fresh produce. Friendly service.

✉ **Emiliano Zapata, corner Benito Juárez** ☎ **(613) 133 0203** ⏱ **Lunch and dinner**

La Paz

El Moro ($)

Beachfront restaurant on road towards Pichilingue peninsula. Wide choice, including seafood, salads.

✉ **2.5 Km Carretera Pichilingue** ☎ **(612) 125 2828** ⏱ **Tue–Sat 8AM–10PM**

Terraza del Perla ($)

Open-air restaurant of an established seafront hotel. Popular for large breakfasts and great snacks at any time.

✉ **Alvaro Obregón 1570** ☎ **(612) 122 0777**

Pacific Mexico

Acapulco

Beto's Condesa ($$)
A popular beachside restaurant. Seafood includes lobster and shrimp specialties, also Mexican and steak dishes. Live music and great views.
✉ **Playa Condesa, Costera Miguel Alemán** ☎ **(744) 484 0473** 🕐 **Noon–midnight**

Carlos 'n Charlie's ($–$$)
This well-known resort chain serves decent food at reasonable prices. Lively atmosphere, loud rock music, and fast service.
✉ **Costera Miguel Alemán 112, near the El Presidente Hotel** ☎ **(744) 484 0089** 🕐 **6PM–late**

Coyuca 22 ($$$)
Unique hilltop setting with fabulous bay views. Superlative international cuisine, professional service. Elegant dress required. Reservations essential.
✉ **Carretera Las Brisas** ☎ **(744) 483 5030** 🕐 **Nov–Apr only**

Raffaello ($–$$)
Branch of a popular Mexico City Italian restaurant. Home-made pasta, Caesar salad, fresh oysters, and seafood dishes. Friendly service.
✉ **Costera Miguel Alemán 1221** ☎ **(744) 484 0100** 🕐 **Dec–Apr, Jul, Aug**

Mazatlán

Doney ($)
Reasonably priced local restaurant, popular for extended lunches. Traditional Mexican dishes, seafood, steaks. Attractive décor includes old local photos.
✉ **Mariano Escobedo 610, corner Cinco de Mayo** ☎ **(669) 981 2651** 🕐 **8AM–10:30PM**

El Parador Español ($–$$)
Spanish cuisine and seafood specialties. Popular, lively place with good service.
✉ **Avenida Camarón Sábalo, next to El Cid** ☎ **(669) 983 0767** 🕐 **7AM–midnight**

El Patio ($$)
Good lobster, steak and Mexican dishes; extensive wine list. Comfortable, rustic setting with outdoor eating and live music in evenings.
✉ **Avenida del Mar 30** ☎ **(669) 981 7301** 🕐 **8AM–2AM**

El Shrimp Bucket ($)
More fun in the evening when live *marimba* music enlivens the atmosphere. Mainly seafood; outdoor dining, great sea views.
✉ **Olas Altas 11** ☎ **(669) 981 6350** 🕐 **6AM–11PM**

Puerto Vallarta

Archie's Wok ($$)
Delicious Thai and Chinese specialties include garlic shrimp, Changmai fish, and numerous vegetarian dishes.
✉ **Francisca Rodríguez 130, near Playa Los Muertos** ☎ **(322) 222 0411** 🕐 **2–11PM. Closed Sun**

La Palapa ($$)
Vallarta's original beachfront restaurant. Excellent seafood menu. Great position and ambience, candle-lit dinners.
✉ **Calle Pulpito on Playa Los Muertos** ☎ **(322) 222 5225** 🕐 **Daily 8AM–11PM**

Red Cabbage Café ($–$$)
Unusual décor plastered with photos of art, film and literary heroes and heroines. Friendly atmosphere and imaginative dishes.
✉ **Riviera del Rio 204A** ☎ **(322) 223 0411** 🕐 **5–11PM**

Seafood
With nearly 10,000km (6,210 miles) of coastline in Mexico, it's not surprising that seafood features prominently on every menu. *Ceviche*, a popular starter, is made of chopped raw fish marinated in lime juice and further flavored with chopped chilli and tomato. This can be delicious but should only be eaten in reputable restaurants. *Camarones* (shrimps) are another favorite, often simply grilled and served with a squeeze of lime or, *al mojo de ajo* (fried in garlic).

The South

From Iguanas to Flowers

Oaxaca is one of the states where culinary imagination takes off. If you are not sampling iguana (served in a stew and with a taste and texture resembling chicken), it may be one of the many Oaxacan variations on the squash theme. Zucchini flowers are a great delicacy, while young squash vines are made into a popular soup. A relative of the squash is the *chayote*, a pear-shaped vegetable grown on a vine that comes into its own, when combined with garlic, tomato or chilli.

Huatulco

Café Huatulco ($)
The place to go when you want a decent coffee. Pretty kiosk in leafy main square that serves real espresso and other coffee specialties. Coffee beans come straight from the hills behind.
✉ **Kiosko de Santa Cruz, Plaza Principal, Santa Cruz** ☎ **(958) 587 0339** ⏰ **9:30AM–11PM**

Oasis Café ($)
A popular spot on the main square. Seafood, grilled meats, salads, sushi. Dine inside or out.
✉ **Bugambilla, corner Flamboyant, La Crucecita** ☎ **(958) 587 0045** ⏰ **7AM–midnight**

Ven Aca ($$)
A comfortable, relaxed restaurant and piano bar.
✉ **Juarez, downtown Santa Cruz** ☎ **(958) 1691** ⏰ **8PM–midnight**

Oaxaca

El Asador Vasco ($$)
Out of this world Mexican cuisine, with a touch of the continental. Centrally located near the city's lively, colorful *zocalo*.
✉ **Portal de Flores** ☎ **(951) 514 4755** ⏰ **1PM–11PM**

Café del Instituto de Artes Gráficas ($)
Oaxaca's most peaceful patio for a shady, light, cheap lunch. Oaxacan specialties (*tortas*, *tostadas*), fresh juices, coffee with mint.
✉ **Alcala 507** ☎ **(951) 516 6980** ⏰ **Breakfast, lunch till 7:30PM**

Los Patos ($$)
Romantic patio restaurant; the upper terrace has close-up views of Santo Domingo. Oaxacan specialties, full bar; contemporary paintings from adjoining art gallery.
✉ **Constitución 104** ☎ **(951) 516 1704** ⏰ **1PM–11PM**

El Topil ($$)
Family-run restaurant serving hearty Oaxacan meat dishes and delicious soups. Friendly atmosphere, though service can be slow.
✉ **Plazuela Labastida 104** ☎ **(951) 514 1617** ⏰ **7:30PM–11PM**

Puerto Ángel

Restaurant Susy ($)
Pleasant beachfront spot with tables under shady *palapas*. Ultra-fresh lobster, oysters, fish and *ceviche*, as well as generous fruit salads.
✉ **Playa del Panteon** ☎ **(958) 584 0319**

San Cristóbal

Café La Selva ($)
Elegant coffee-house in contemporary style. Excellent coffee in all forms, snacks, cakes; newspapers.
✉ **Avenida Cresencio Rosas, corner Cuauhtémoc** ☎ **(967) 678 7243**

Veracruz

Gran Café del Portal ($)
Stunning old coffee house and restaurant, once known as La Parroquía. Still has its original 1810 period décor.
✉ **Independencia, corner Zamora** ☎ **(228) 813 2751** ⏰ **Daily 6AM–midnight**

La Fuente de Mariscos ($$)
A wide variety of fresh seafood from the Atlantic. Live rock and salsa bands.
✉ **Hernán Cortés 1524** ☎ **(228) 818 2412** ⏰ **Long lunches only**

The Yucatán Peninsula

Campeche

Restaurant Miramar ($$)
One of Campeche's best seafood restaurants, near the port.
✉ **Calle 8 y 61** ☎ **(981) 816 2883** 🕐 **Daily 11–3, 6–10:30**

Cancún

Los Almendros ($$)
Classic Yucatecan fare such as *poc chuc* and *cochinita pibil*. Live trio music in evening. In downtown area.
✉ **Avenida Bonampak, corner Avenida Sayil** ☎ **(798) 887 1332** 🕐 **10:30AM–11PM**

Captain's Cove ($$)
Palapa restaurant overlooking lagoon. Ultra-fresh seafood specialties, barbecued meats and Mexican dishes. Happy hour 4–7PM.
✉ **Boulevard Kukulcán, Km 9.5** ☎ **(998) 885 0016** 🕐 **Daily 7AM–11PM**

La Dolce Vita ($$$)
Excellent Italian cuisine: fresh pasta, seafood, salads. Attentive service. Booking advisable.
✉ **Boulevard Kukulcán, Km 14.6, opposite Hotel Marriott** ☎ **(998) 885 0150** 🕐 **Lunch and dinner**

Cozumel

Lobster's Cove ($$–$$$)
Chic restaurant on sea-front, south of main square. Lobster, pasta, seafood, and flambéed desserts. Live music in the evenings.
✉ **Avenida Rafael Melgar 790, between Calle 9 and 11 Sur** ☎ **(987) 872 4022** 🕐 **Daily noon–11PM**

La Veranda ($$$)
The restaurant is in a pretty, traditional, wooden building. There's a great garden and the cuisine is mostly Caribbean.
✉ **4 Norte 140, at Avenue 5a and 10a** ☎ **(987) 872 4132** 🕐 **Daily 6PM–10:30PM**

Isla Mujeres

Zazil-Ha ($$)
Romantic outdoor setting in hotel garden. Wide-ranging menu includes salads, seafood, pasta, and meat dishes. Good bar with 7–9PM happy hour.
✉ **Playa Norte** ☎ **(998) 887 0279** 🕐 **Daily 7:30AM–10PM**

Mérida

Los Almendros ($$)
Famous Yucatecan restaurant. Fine choice of local specialties; regional show on Fridays at 7.
✉ **Calle 50-A No 493, Plaza de la Mejorada** ☎ **(999) 923 8135** 🕐 **Daily 9AM–11PM**

Café la Habana ($)
Serves great breakfasts, Cuban sandwiches, soups and Yucatecan snacks, coffee, beer, and liquors. Great for people watching.
✉ **Corner of 59th and 62nd** ☎ **(999) 928 6502** 🕐 **24 hours**

Playa del Carmen

Blue Lobster ($$)
A *palapa*-roofed restaurant with sea views. Serves lobster, seafood, pasta, meat dishes and flambéed desserts.
✉ **Avenida 5, between Calle 4 and 6** ☎ **(987) 873 1360** 🕐 **7AM–11PM**

La Parilla ($–$$)
Established, popular restaurant on Playa's main drag. Salads, seafood, Mexican dishes.
✉ **Avenida 5, corner Calle 8** ☎ **(987) 873 0687** 🕐 **7AM–1AM**

Yucatecan Cuisine

Unique in Mexico due to its prolonged isolation, Yucatecan cuisine combines influences from Europe (particularly France), New Orleans and Cuba. Common dishes include *sopa de lima*, a delicious chicken broth of shredded chicken, *tortilla* and lime juice; *pollo* or *cochinita pibil*, chicken or pork marinaded in spices and sour orange juice then baked in banana leaves; and *poc chuc*, pork fillet marinated in sour orange juice and served with pickled onions. Another popular ingredient is *pavo*, wild turkey, which can be shredded, wrapped in *tortillas*, pickled or stewed in soups.

Central Mexico

Price-Categories

Approximate price for a double room with attached shower or bathroom per night:

$ = $120 – 250 (pesos)
$$ = $250 – 600 (pesos)
$$$ = $600 (pesos) upwards

In beach resorts, walk-in prices rocket in high season (Dec–Apr), so add on about 30 percent to the above categories.

Mexico City

La Casona ($$$)

Luxury boutique-style hotel, set in the heart of the city. Excellent service, beautiful furnishings.

✉ Durango 280 ☎ (55) 5286 3001; fax: (55) 5211 0871 🚇 Sevilla

Hotel de Cortés ($$)

Legendary hotel in former 18th-century hospice. Courtyard restaurant; can be noisy but in a good location.

✉ Hidalgo 85, Centro ☎ (55) 5518 2181; fax: (55) 5512 1863 🚇 Hidalgo

Hotel Gillow ($)

Large hotel in heart of the historic center. The interior lacks charm but rooms are comfortable and good value.

✉ Isabel La Católica, Centro ☎ (55) 5518 1440/6 🚇 Allende

Hotel Majestic ($$)

Plum location overlooking *Zócalo*. Colonial-style décor, terrace restaurant. Part of Best Western group.

✉ Madero 73, Centro ☎ (55) 5521 8600; fax: (55) 5512 6262 🚇 Zócalo

Hotel Maria Cristina ($$)

Charming colonial hotel with gardens, patio, piano bar, restaurant, and plenty of atmosphere. Book ahead. Just north of Zona Rosa.

✉ Río Lerma 31 ☎ (55) 5566 9194 🚇 Insurgentes

Vasco de Quiroga ($$)

Friendly family hotel on quieter, eastern side of Zona Rosa. Fifty colonial-style rooms. Restaurant.

✉ Londres 15, Zona Rosa ☎ (55) 5546 2614; fax: (55) 5535 2257 🚇 Insurgentes

Cuernavaca

Hotel Bajo El Volcán ($$)

Well-appointed, centrally located hotel whose name refers to Malcolm Lowry's book. Parking, pool, bar, restaurant.

✉ Alejandro de Humboldt ☎ (777) 312 4873

Hotel Las Hortensias ($)

In a very central location with modest but clean and adequate rooms opening on to pretty garden courtyard.

✉ Hidalgo 22 ☎ (777) 318 5265; fax: (777) 312 3061

Guadalajara

Hotel Frances ($$)

Popular, historic old hotel close to Plaza de la Liberación. Inside patio, restaurant, bar, antiques. Comfortable modernized rooms.

✉ Maestranza 35 ☎ (33) 3613 1190

Plaza Génova ($)

Well-located modern hotel. Good value, comfortable rooms; clean.

✉ Avenida Juárez 123 ☎ (33) 3613 7500; fax: (55) 3614 8253

Guanajuato

Hotel San Diego ($$)

Popular hotel overlooking the historic town's main square. Reasonable rooms and a restaurant.

✉ Jardín de la Unión 1 ☎ (473) 732 1300

Posada Santa Fé ($$)

Elegant mansion with antique furnishings and well-appointed rooms. The Posada Santa Fé also boasts an excellent restaurant with outside tables on main square. Parking available.

✉ Plaza Principal 12 ☎ (473) 732 0084; fax: (473) 732 4653

Jalapa
Posada del Cafeto ($)
Attractively decorated little hotel down a peaceful side street. Cheerful, fresh rooms but rather surly service.
✉ Canovas 12 ☎ (228) 817 0023

Morelia
Hotel Casino ($$)
Reasonably priced hotel overlooking main square and cathedral. Colonial style, good amenities, popular outdoor café under arches.
✉ Portal Hidalgo 229 ☎ (443) 313 1053/1101

Pátzcuaro
Hotel Los Escudos ($)
Elegant hotel on scenic main square. Well-appointed rooms surround leafy patios. Popular restaurant. Parking.
✉ Portal Hidalgo 73 ☎ (434) 342 0138

Puebla
Hotel Colonial ($–$$)
Modernized colonial hotel on main square. Small but reasonable rooms.
✉ Calle 4 Sur 105 ☎ (222) 246 4612; fax: 246 0818

Hotel Posada San Pedro ($$)
Family hotel with good rooms and pool. Very central.
✉ Avenue 2, OTE No 202 ☎ (222) 246 5077

Querétaro
Hotel Impala ($$)
Modern hotel overlooking Parque Alameda. Decent rooms but front ones are noisy. Restaurant, parking.
✉ Colón 1, Centro ☎ (442) 212 2570; fax: 212 4515

Hotel Mesón de Santa Rosa ($$)
Attractive colonial-style hotel on main square with patio restaurant. Upper end of price category, good value.
✉ Pasteur Sur 17, Centro ☎ (442) 224 2623, fax: 125522

La Casa de la Marquesa ($$$)
One of Querétaro's most beautiful mansions. Luxurious, individually decorated suites, exotically furnished with antiques. Part of Small Luxury Hotels of the World group.
✉ Madero 41, Centro ☎ (442) 212 0092; fax: 212 0098

San Miguel del Allende
Hotel Posada de San Francisco ($$)
Excellent colonial-style hotel. Small but well-furnished rooms with heating. Restaurant in front courtyard.
✉ Plaza Principal 2 ☎ (415) 152 0072

Mansion Virreyes ($$)
Small but nicely furnished rooms surrounding a courtyard. Good restaurant. Rates include breakfast.
✉ Canal 19 ☎ (415) 152 3355

Posada de las Monjas ($–$$)
Converted monastery with comfortable rooms in a peaceful but central location. Friendly and popular. Restaurant, parking.
✉ Calle Canal 37 ☎ (415) 152 0171; fax: 152 6277

Taxco
Hotel Agua Escondida ($)
In a good location; rooms on the main square with terrace views of the cathedral. Rooftop pool, good children's facilities, parking.
✉ Plaza Borda 4 ☎ (762) 622 1166; fax: (762) 622 1306

Hotel Posada San Javier ($)
Excellent value 19-room hotel surrounding palm-shaded garden in central location. Rustic furnishings, balconies. Small pool, garage.
✉ Ex-Rastro 4, Estacas 1 ☎ (762) 622 3177; fax: 622 2351

Colonial Hotels
Central Mexico is the best area to experience the atmosphere of converted colonial mansions or haciendas. The latter are often outside town and high-priced, so not always suitable, but many of the former are very affordable. On top of this, their historic background puts them in the heart of town and, at best, on the *zócalo* or main square. Check rooms before registering to ensure the noise level is not too high.

The North & Baja California

Margarita
For once this is not a reference to Mexico's favorite cocktail but the name of a dynamic guest-house owner in Creel, along the Copper Canyon route. For years backpackers were hauled off the Chihuahua–Pacifico train to stay at her expansive and friendly guest house, indulging in generous communal meals before being whisked around the canyons by members of her extended family. Today, her operation has expanded considerably and no traveler will find themselves without a bed for the night.

Barranca del Cobre (Copper Canyon)
Hotel Divisadero Barrancas ($–$$)
Spectacularly sited, looking over Urique canyon. Good rooms with satellite TV, restaurant, bar, parking.
✉ **Divisadero Barrancas Km 622, Urique** ☎ **(635) 415 1199**

Los Cabos
Esperanza Resort ($$$+)
Perhaps the most dramatic view of Cabo's famed landmark "El Arco" is from Esperanza, a plush, luxurious collection of 50 suites and six villas. Located at exclusive and exceptional Punta Ballena.
✉ **Trans. Highway Km 7, Cabo San Lucas** ☎ **(624) 145 6400**

Chihuahua
Hotel San Francisco ($$)
Modern hotel behind the cathedral. Amenities include bar, restaurant, travel desk.
✉ **Victoria 409** ☎ **(614) 416 7550**

Ensenada
El Cid Hotel ($$)
Small-scale, Best Western hotel close to the bay. Strong accent on Mexican décor. Restaurant, bar, pool, parking.
✉ **Avenida López Mateos 993** ☎ **(646) 178 2401**

Loreto
Hotel Mision de Loreto ($)
Attractively designed hotel overlooking sea. Spacious rooms with air-conditioning. Large pool, bar, parking.
✉ **Boulevard López Mateos 1** ☎ **(613) 135 0048**

Hotel La Pinta ($$)
Good standard air-conditioned rooms complete with satellite TV. Attractive pool with *palapas* and sea view; restaurant, bar, parking.
✉ **Calle Francisco Madero, Playa Loreto** ☎ **(613) 135 0025**

Mulegé
Vieja Hacienda ($)
Historic, atmospheric hacienda where John Wayne once sipped margaritas. Wonderful courtyard.
✉ **Calle Romero Rubio** ☎ **(612) 153 0021**

La Paz
Hotel Club El Moro ($)
Pleasant, friendly hotel across road from sea; air-conditioned rooms with satellite TV and balconies surrounding small pool.
✉ **Km 2 Carretera Pichilingue, Colonia Colina del Sol** ☎ **(612) 122 4084**

La Posada de Engelbert ($$)
Nicely designed, low-rise beachfront hotel in lovely gardens. Spacious rooms and villas with air-conditioning and satellite TV. Restaurant, bar with live music.
✉ **Nueva Reforma, corner Playa Sur** ☎ **(612) 122 4011**

San Felipe
Hotel Las Misiones San Felipe ($$)
Modern hotel with some good views. Comfortable rooms. Pool, bar, parking.
✉ **Avenida Misión Loreto 148, Playa San Felipe** ☎ **(686) 577 1280**

San Ignacio
Posada San Ignacio ($)
Good-value, friendly hotel with comfortable rooms. Organizes cave-painting and whale-watching tours.
✉ **Avenida Venustiano Carranza 2** ☎ **(615) 154 0313**

Pacific Mexico

Acapulco

Hotel Elcano Royal ($$$)
Opposite golf course at eastern end of Costera, with pool over-looking beach. Spacious rooms, excellent restaurant, bars, good service.

✉ **Avenida Costera Miguel Alemán** ☎ **(744) 484 1950**

Hotel Los Flamingos ($)
Tranquil old 1930s hotel once frequented by Cary Grant and Errol Flynn. Lovely garden, pool, air-conditioned rooms, good restaurant, parking, tour desk.

✉ **Avenida Adolfo López Mateos, Las Playas** ☎ **(744) 482 0690**

Ixtapa-Zihuatanejo

Hotel Fiesta Mexicana ($$)
Beside the palm-fringed beach of La Ropa, a comfortable hotel with pool, tennis, coffee shop, and tour desk.

✉ **Playa La Ropa, Zihuatanejo** ☎ **(755) 554 3636**

Hotel Irma ($$)
Comfortable, well-run hotel with air-conditioned rooms high on the hillside over-looking the beach. Tennis, pool, coffee shop, tours.

✉ **La Madera, Playa La Madera, Zihuatanejo** ☎ **(755) 554 2105**

Hotel Posada Real ($$)
Good family-style seafront hotel with air-conditioned rooms, pool, children's playground, tennis, restaurant, bar, boat tours.

✉ **Boulevard Ixtapa, Ixtapa** ☎ **(755) 553 1745**

Mazatlán

Hotel Azteca Inn ($$)
Friendly hotel. Well-furnished rooms with satellite TV, some overlooking pool. Bar, coffee shop, parking.

✉ **Rodolfo T Loalza 307** ☎ **(669) 913 4477**

Hotel Costa de Oro ($$)
Oceanside hotel with rooms arranged around inner patios, gardens, pool, and open-air restaurant. Tennis, tours.

✉ **Camarón Sábalo, Zona Dorada** ☎ **(669) 913 5113**

Puerto Vallarta

Hotel Quinta Maria Cortez ($$)
A fun, wonderful, maze-like seven-story house with seven suites. Small pool, rooftop terrace and located right on tranquil Conchas Chinas Beach.

✉ **Sagitario 132, Playa Concha Chinas** ☎ **(322) 221 5317**

Hacienda San Angel ($$$)
Romantic collection of three inter-connecting villas with nine suites. One villa, Casa Bursus, was Richard Burton's Puerto Vallarta home. Fantastic location.

✉ **Miramar No. 3367** ☎ **(322) 221 2277**

Hotel Rosita ($$)
Vallarta's first hotel, overlooking main town beach, with clean, simple rooms. Good value for location.

✉ **Miramar No. 336** ☎ **(322) 222 2692**

San Blas

Hotel Garza Canela ($$)
Attractively designed hotel with gardens, pool, excellent restaurant. Spacious rooms. Close to beach; birdwatching tours arranged.

✉ **Paredes Sur 106, Centro** ☎ **(323) 285 0112**

Last Resort Deals

If you are traveling in Mexico and want to stay in a beach resort such as Los Cabos, Puerto Vallarta, or the Copper Canyon, some of the best deals on offer are with the regional airlines such as Aerocalifornia or Mexicana. Check out their flight and hotel offers at any travel agent, they are often cheaper than the return flight itself.

The South

Village Accommodation

A recent initiative set into motion by the state of Oaxaca offers an interesting budget alternative to Oaxaca's colonial-style hotels. Launched under the name of Tourist Yu'u, it is a string of eight purpose-built huts located in villages along the road between the state capital and Mitla. Each one contains four bunk beds, a kitchen and shower room, and is managed by a local villager. These make ideal self-catering bases for families or students, although their location makes hiring a car essential. Contact Sedetur (state tourist office) in Oaxaca for further information ☎ 951 60984, fax: 61500.

Huatulco

Casa del Mar ($$$)

Luxurious suites all with private terrace and ocean views in an isolated spot on a cliff edge. Close to golf course.

✉ **Balcones de Tangolunda** ☎ (958) 581 0203, toll free: 800 908 1142

Hotel Marlin ($$)

This pleasantly sized French-owned hotel, is a few minutes' walk from the beach. Spacious air-conditioned rooms, restaurant, pool, and travel desk. Efficiently run.

✉ **Paseo Mitla 107, Bahía de Santa Cruz** ☎ (958) 587 0055

Oaxaca

Casa Oaxaca ($$$)

Superb eclectic hotel, decorated with exceptional contemporary Mexican taste. Spacious rooms and patios, pool, paintings. Breakfast included in very reasonable rates.

✉ **García Vigil 407** ☎ (951) 514 4173; fax: 516 4412

Hotel Francia ($)

A large 46-room hotel, one block east of the zócalo. Spacious, clean rooms, friendly staff. Can be noisy.

✉ **20 de Noviembre 212** ☎ (951) 516 4811; fax: 516 4251

Puerto Ángel

Buena Vista ($)

Perhaps the best location in Puerto Ángel, on a hillside behind the port. Imaginatively designed, simple rooms, some with balconies and hammocks. Large dining terrace.

✉ **Aptdo Postal 48** ☎ (958) 584 3104

Villa Serena Horencia ($)

Excellent value, Mediterranean-style inn beside fishing beach. Simple rooms with fan and/or air-conditioning. Good restaurant and sun terrace. Friendly atmosphere.

✉ **Virgilio Uribe** ☎ (958) 584 3044

San Cristóbal de las Casas

Hotel Flamboyant Español ($$)

An elegant, colonial-style hotel with well-appointed rooms off flowery patio. Restaurant, bar, gym, solarium.

✉ **Calle 1 de Marzo 15** ☎ (967) 678 0045; fax: 678 0514

Tuxtla Gutiérrez

Gran Hotel Humberto ($-$$)

Large, central 1950s hotel with original furnishings. Good rooms, friendly staff, restaurant.

✉ **Avenida Central Poniente 180** ☎ (961) 612 2504

Veracruz

Hotel El Faro ($)

Family-run hotel tucked away a few streets back from harbor. Simple rooms with TV and air-conditioning or fan.

✉ **16 de Septiembre 223** ☎ (228) 831 6588

Hotel Mocambo ($$)

Well-established favorite on Mocambo beach, about 8km (5 miles) south of town. Decent-sized rooms, some overlooking garden and beach. Pool, tennis court, travel desk, coffee shop.

✉ **Calzada Rúiz Cortines 4000, Colonia Mocambo, Boca del Río** ☎ (228) 822 0333

The Yucatán Peninsula

Campeche

Hotel America ($)

Converted mansion near main square; good-value double rooms, fan, TV. Some rooms still awaiting renovation. Safe parking at nearby Hotel Ramada.

 Calle 10 No 252 ☎ **(981) 816 4588**

Cancún

Few Cancún hotels see walk-in customers. They are best booked on a package basis through a travel agent.

Chichén Itzá

Hotel Hacienda Chichén ($$$)

Lovely 16th-century hacienda hotel with modern air-conditioned cottage accommodation. Beautiful gardens, pool, restaurant.

☒ **Chichén Itzá** ☎ **(985) 851 0045; toll free (800) 624 8451**

Cozumel

Hotel Casa del Mar ($$)

Rustic-style hotel south of San Miguel overlooking ocean with air-conditioned rooms, pool, wet bar, restaurant, gardens.

☒ **Costera Sur, Km 4** ☎ **(987) 872 1900**

Sol Cabañas del Caribe ($$)

Intimate, beachfront hotel with rooms and cabins. Bar, restaurant, and good beach.

☒ **Carretera Costera Norte, Km 5.1** ☎ **(987) 872 0161**

Isla Mujeres

Posada del Mar ($$)

One of Isla's earliest hotels in large garden overlooking sea. Spacious air-conditioned rooms, bright exterior colors, large pool, bar, restaurant. Efficiently run. Central but quiet location.

☒ **Avenida Rueda Medina 15A** ☎ **(998) 877 0044; fax: (998) 877 0266**

Mérida

Gran Hotel ($$)

Fabulous 1902 hotel with elegant, spacious rooms. All open on to a veranda surrounding leafy inner patio. Friendly and good value. Restaurant, parking.

☒ **Calle 60 No 496, Parque Cepada** ☎ **(999) 924 7730**

Hotel Casa del Balam ($$$)

Stylish central hotel in modernized 19th-century building. Soundproofing, pool, colonial features, satellite TV, travel agency, parking.

☒ **Calle 60 No 488** ☎ **(999) 924 2150**

Playa del Carmen

Blue Parrot Inn ($$–$$$)

Established, hip favorite on beachfront. Variety of rooms, bungalows and *palapa* huts. Popular bar with live music; massages, restaurant.

☒ **Calle 12 Norte** ☎ **(987) 873 0083**

Hotel Lunato ($$)

Intimate hotel on Avenida 5. Rooms finished to a high standard.

☒ **Avenida 5 Norte, between Calle 6 and 8** ☎ **(987) 873 0884**

Tulum

Ana y José ($$)

Palapa roofed cottages on a quiet beach. Good diving.

☒ **Km 7 Carretero Boca Paila** ☎ **(984) 880 6022**

Hotel Boca Paila ($$)

Nine room hotel/fishing lodge known for its permit, tarpon and snook fishing.

☒ **Laguna Boca Paila** ☎ **(800) 245 1950**

Split Personality

As far as accommodation is concerned, the Yucatán peninsula is neatly divided into two halves. To the east is the Cancún-Tulum Corridor, where walk-in prices match the popularity and services. To the west are relaxed towns with a life outside tourism such as Valladolid (► 90), Campeche (► 86) and even Mérida (► 84). These, together with smaller places near by, offer excellent value both for food and hotels.

Markets

Markets

Many large towns have weekly markets that often bring streams of local people into the plaza. If you have already visited a few crafts shops to get an idea of what is commonly available and you see something exceptional in a market, buy it! You may not see it again.
Bargaining is part of any transaction, but remember how impoverished most of these people are.

Central Mexico

Mexico City
Bazar Sábado

Upscale handicrafts bazaar in the southern San Ángel neighborhood spills onto pavements. Few bargains in silver, ceramics, glass, clothing, and textiles, but a lively atmosphere.

✉ **Plaza San Jacinto 11, San Ángel** ⏰ **Sat only 10–7** 🚌 **San Ángel *pesero* bus down Insurgentes**

La Ciudadela

An open-air treasure trove of handicrafts from all over the country surrounds a central courtyard. Bargaining is essential.

✉ **Mercado de las Artesanías, Plaza de la Ciudadela, Calle Balderas** ⏰ **Mon–Sat 11–6, Sun 11–2** 🚇 **Juárez or Balderas**

Guanajuato
Mercado Hidalgo

Superb turn-of-the-century iron-and-glass market building in town center with food market on ground floor and upstairs stalls selling baskets, embroidered clothes, pottery, shawls, and more.

✉ **Avenida Juárez** ⏰ **Mon–Sat 9–6**

Morelia
Casa de las Artesanías

A vast handicrafts emporium located in a former convent. Wide choice of Michoacán lacquerware, woodcarvings, pottery, copper and furniture. Small museum on premises. Shipping arranged. Market stalls in plaza outside.

✉ **Ex-Convento de San Francisco, Plaza Valladolid** ☎ **(443) 312 2486** ⏰ **Daily 10–3, 5–8**

Puebla
Mercado La Victoria

Central market next to Santo Domingo church. Upper floor offers Pueblan food specialties and wide range of handicrafts from the region. Some upscale craft shops on ground level.

✉ **Calle 5 de Mayo, between Avenida 8 and 6** ⏰ **Mon–Sat 10:30–8**

The South

Oaxaca
Mercado de Artesanías

Large crafts market southwest of the *zócalo*. Rugs, textiles, jewelry, painted wooden animals, and ceramics dominate. Bargaining essential.

✉ **Zaragoza, corner J P García** ⏰ **Daily 11–8**

San Cristóbal de las Casas
Mercado José Castillo Tielmans

The main indigenous market for surrounding villages. Fabulous crafts and ethnic variety.

✉ **Avenida General Utrilla, corner Nicaragua** ⏰ **Daily 6–3 (except Sun)**

The Yucatán Peninsula

Mérida
Mercado Municipal de Artesanías

A sprawling crafts market in two separate buildings. Mayan embroidered dresses, lace, hammocks, shellware, Panama hats. Prices are exorbitant and demand hard bargaining.

✉ **Calle 65, corner Calle 56, behind post office (*Correos*)** ⏰ **Daily 8AM–9PM**

Art & Antiques

Central Mexico

Mexico City
Plaza San Angel
Mexico City's largest antiques center. Furniture, paintings, decorative arts, silver, bric-à-brac. Weekend market stalls bring the area alive; watch out for copies.
✉ **Plaza del Angel, Londres 161 and Hamburgo 150, Zona Rosa** 🕒 **Daily 10–8; antiques market Sat–Sun 10–4**
🚇 **Insurgentes**

Puebla
Casa Poblana
Attractively renovated building in heart of Puebla's antique district, near the Sunday antiques market of Plazuela de los Sapos. Contemporary home objects (glass, ceramics, wood) beside unusual antiques.
✉ **Calle 6 Sur 406** ☎ **(222) 242 0848**

San Miguel del Allende
Bazar Unicornio
Large courtyard with unusual selection of antiques, hand-painted ex-votos, crosses in embossed silver, and other religious objects.
✉ **Hernández Macías 80** ☎ **(415) 152 1306**

Pacific Mexico

Puerto Vallarta
Galería Museo Huichol
Large gallery specializing in Huichol art and crafts, giving direct support to the crafts-people. Demonstrations.
✉ **Morelos 490** ☎ **(322) 222 0182**

Galería Uno
Contemporary art gallery in attractive converted house.

Paintings, sculptures, graphics, and posters by well-known Mexican artists.
✉ **Morelos 561** ☎ **(322) 222 0908** 🕒 **Mon–Sat 10–8**

Olinala Gallery
Well-displayed choice selection of fine indigenous art. Ritual masks, Huichol beadwork, lapidary work, and other rare original pieces.
✉ **Lázaro Cárdenas 274** ☎ **(322) 222 4995** 🕒 **Mon–Sat 10–2, 5–9PM**

The South

Huatulco
Galerías Huatulco
Contemporary works (paintings and sculptures) by artists from Oaxaca, Morelos, Michoacán and Jalisco. Also sells interesting jewelry designs in gold and silver.
✉ **Hotel Sheraton, Tangolunda** ☎ **(958) 581 0080** 🕒 **Mon–Sat 9–1, 5–7, Sun 9–2**

Oaxaca
Galería Gráfica Soruco
Interesting selection of works on paper, and photos.
✉ **Plazuela Labastida 104C** ☎ **(951) 514 3938**

Galería Quetzalli
Large contemporary art gallery showing best of young Oaxacan artists. Combined with a bar-restaurant.
✉ **Constitución 104** ☎ **(951) 514 2606**

La Mano Mágica
Long-established Oaxacan art gallery with regular exhibitions of contemporary artists and rug designs. Adjoining handicrafts store.
✉ **Alcalá 203** ☎ **(951) 516 4275**

Archaeological Artefacts
Remember that it is strictly prohibited to export any pre-Hispanic artefact from Mexico. Countless vendors, particularly on archaeological sites, attempt to fob off ready-made "artifacts" as the real thing. Buy one if you like it, but only pay its real handicraft value. Large stores and museums sell the best-quality copies.

Handicrafts

Pottery and Ceramics

Mexican craftspeople make an extraordinary variety of pottery and ceramics. Pueblan Talavera has the most refined traditional patterns, Michoacán the most extraordinary shapes, San Bartolomé, in Oaxaca, a unique metallic black range, and Dolores Hidalgo, near Guanajuato, colorful cheap designs. Beware of using the heavier ceramics fired at low temperatures for food, as they have a dangerously high lead content that is easily absorbed.

Central Mexico

Mexico City

Avalos Brothers

One hundred years of glass blowing experience, and you can watch them at work next to the store. Prices are generally good—they see few tourists.

✉ Carretones 5, Centro Historico ☎ (55) 5522 5311 🕐 Mon–Fri 10–5

Fonart

Three branches of this state-run handicrafts store promise top-quality goods. You'll find excellent carved wooden furniture, pottery, ceramics, glass, textiles, jewelry, basket-ware, and more. Shipping arranged, fixed prices. The largest choice is at Patriotismo branch.

✉ Avenida Patriotismo 691, Mixcoac. Also at Avenida Juárez 89, Centro; Presidente Carranza 115, Coyoacán ☎ (55) 5563 4060 🕐 Mon–Sat 9–9, Sun 10–7 🚇 Mixcoac (main branch)

La Luna Descalza

Good selection and imaginative display of handicrafts from all over Mexico. Lots of decorative tinwork. Near Bazar Sábado.

✉ Plaza San Jacinto 3, San Ángel ☎ (55) 5616 4617 🚌 San Ángel *pesero* bus down Insurgentes

Cuernavaca

Casillas Artesanías

Good selection of handmade furnishing items and handicrafts from the states of Michoacán, Guanajuato, Jalisco, Puebla, and Oaxaca.

✉ San Diego 805, Colonia Vista Hermosa ☎ (777) 316 3598 🕐 Daily

Cerámica Santa María

Demonstrates and sells handpainted pottery. Techniques and designs developed over 40 years.

✉ Zapata 900, Centro ☎ (777) 313 0670

Guanajuato

Casa de Artesanía

Reasonable variety of crafts from central Mexico in store located by historic hacienda outside town.

✉ Ex-Hacienda San Gabriel de Barrera, Marfil ☎ (473) 772 2408 🕐 Wed–Sun 10–5

Fonart

Wide selection of Mexican handicrafts at this state-owned store. Fixed prices and top quality.

✉ Casa del Conde de la Valenciana, Km 5 ☎ (473) 772 2550 🕐 Daily 10–6

Puebla

Uriarte

Renowned workshop and outlet for traditional Talavera ceramics, founded in 1824. Exquisitely hand-painted pieces, but expensive. Short tours of workshops.

✉ Avenida 4 Poniente 911, between Calle 9 and 11 ☎ (222) 232 1598 🕐 Mon–Sat 10–6, Sun 11–6:30

Querétaro

Casa Queretana de Las Artesanías

Sells a wide range of local craftwork and interior decoration items. Lace, bed and table linen, pottery, wooden furniture.

✉ Andador Libertad 52, Centro ☎ (442) 214 1235 🕐 Daily

Florería Encanto

Large store with good selection of reasonably

priced pottery from Dolores Hidalgo and glassware from Guadalajara.

✉ **Pasteur Sur 29** ☎ **(442) 212 3737**

Fonart
Dependable state-owned handicrafts store with items from all over the country. Policy aims to give artisans better prices.

✉ **Angela Peralta 20, Centro**
☎ **(442) 212 2648**

San Miguel de Allende
Bazar Romero & Flores
Large store opposite Instituto Allende with wide choice of metal lamps in copper, brass or perforated tin. Wrought-iron candle-holders, hand-blown glass.

✉ **Ancha de San Antonio 13**
☎ **(415) 152 7274**

Casa del Inquisidor
Historic house converted into labyrinthine arts, crafts, and home furnishings store.

✉ **Cuadrante 36** ☎ **(415) 152 1325**

Taxco
Gezem
Colonia-style emporium, selling a range of handicrafts and silver.

✉ **Benito Juarez 82** ☎ **(762) 622 7539**

The North and Baja California

Los Cabos
Casa Mexicana
Wide selection of Mexican handicrafts from Talavera pottery to wooden furniture.

✉ **Main plaza, Avenida Cabo San Lucas, Cabo San Lucas**
☎ **(624) 143 1933** 🕐 **Daily 4–10PM**

Copal
Attractively converted old house with fine selection of handicrafts from all over Mexico. Taxco silver, hand-

blown glass, rattan furniture, masks, rugs, pottery.

✉ **Plaza Mijares 10, San José del Cabo** ☎ **(624) 142 3070**

Pacific Mexico

Puerto Vallarta
Quetzalcóatl
Spacious emporium of indigenous art such as beaded Huichol pieces, black pottery from Oaxaca, Aztec and Maya reproductions, masks and terracotta sculptures. Shipping for large or delicate items.

✉ **Juárez 428** ☎ **(322) 223 2380** 🕐 **Mon–Sat 9:30–8:30**

Shapes
Interesting store and functioning workshop making reproductions of Paquimé pottery in all shapes and sizes.

✉ **Aquíles Serdán 406**
☎ **(322) 222 3890**

The South

Oaxaca
Arte y Tradicion
Co-operative established by several villages working together, each selling their own produce.

✉ **Garcia Vigil 406** ☎ **(951) 516 3552**

La Casa de la Iguana
Lizards are the central theme here, but they also sell many other unusual items from all over Mexico. Furniture and lamps too.

✉ **Allende 109** ☎ **(951) 516 0588**

Mujeres Artesanas de las Regiones de Oaxaca
Sprawling showroom/store displaying craftswork by a local women's co-operative. Pottery, woodcarvings, weaving, embroidered clothes, leatherwork, and much more. Packaging.

✉ **Calle 5 de Mayo 204**
☎ **(951) 516 0670**

Siesta Time
When you are in southern Mexico and coastal resorts, forget about shopping in the afternoon. This is siesta or beach time. Most shops open around 9AM, then close at 1 or 2 for lunch, reopening at 4 or 5 and staying open until 8 or 9.

Clothing & Accessories

Fashion Buys

If you are not taken by westernized Mexican fashion, traditional clothes, shawls, and textiles, buy something original. Intricately embroidered textiles from Oaxaca and Chiapas are now collector's items, but a *guayabera* (a loose-fitting man's shirt) from the Yucatán will not break the bank, nor will a handwoven *serape* (shawl), unless it is silk. Leather belts come in countless designs and are great bargains.

Central Mexico

Mexico City
Casa Cuesta
Good quality, ready-made men's clothing and tailoring in fabrics ranging from cashmere to silk. Not cheap.
✉ **Río Sena 87a, across Reforma from Zona Rosa** ☎ **(55) 5208 1607** Ⓜ **Cuauhtémoc**

Zara
Stylish clothes usually in synthetic blends, made in Spain and sometimes reasonably priced. Bags, shoes and accessories too.
✉ **Madero 50, corner Isabel La Católica, Centro Histórico** ☎ **(55) 5525 1516** Ⓜ *Zócalo* **or Allende**

San Miguel de Allende
El Sombrero
Handmade straw and leather hats. Special orders made at San Francisco 30.
✉ **San Francisco 14** ☎ **(415) 152 3675**

The North and Baja California

Los Cabos
La Sandia
Stylish women's clothes, accessories and jewelry inspired by pre-Hispanic designs.
✉ **Plaza Míjares 6-B, San José del Cabo** ☎ **(624) 142 2230**

Pacific Mexico

Acapulco
Armando's
Light cotton women's jackets, dresses and other summerwear in clear, tropical colors, often finely embroidered.

✉ **Costera Miguel Alemán 1252–7** ☎ **(744) 484 5111**

Esteban
Renowned local designer makes casual and evening wear for men and women to order. Ready-to-wear collection and accessories.
✉ **Costera Miguel Alemán 2010** ☎ **(774) 484 3084**

Mazatlán
Gaby's Leather Factory
Understated-looking factory outlet offering good bargains in leather clothes and accessories for men and women. Made-to-measure within the day.
✉ **Camarón Sábalo 1652** ☎ **(669) 916 1022**

The South

Huatulco
Ay Caramba! Kanoa Boutique
Casual sportswear and beach clothing.
✉ **Hotel Flamboyant, Plaza Principal, La Crucecita** ☎ **(958) 587 0244**

Oaxaca
Dishvé
A change from Oaxaca's indigenous embroidered clothes. Cheesecloth and cotton women's wear, some accessories. See next door too.
✉ **Plaza Santo Domingo, Alcalá 407** ☎ **(951) 514 2913**

The Yucatán Peninsula

Isla Mujeres
Qué Barbara
Unusual designs from Guatemala, mainly for women.
✉ **Calle Matamoros 18** ☎ **(987) 877 0705**

Jewelry

Central Mexico

Mexico City
Bazar del Centro
Attractive jewelry emporium specializing in pearls and loose semi-precious and precious stones.
✉ **Isabel la Católica 30, Centro Histórico** ☎ **(55) 5510 1840**
Ⓜ **Pino Suárez**

Talleres de los Ballesteros
Jewelry, tableware and other decorative items in sterling silver.
✉ **Amberes 24, Zona Rosa**
☎ **(55) 5511 8281** Ⓜ
Insurgentes

Puebla
La Bella Elena
Unusual silver and amber jewelry designs. Near the Sunday antiques market on Plazuela de los Sapos. Upstairs café-bar.
✉ **Calle 6 Sur 310** ☎ **(222) 242 0702**

Taxco
Platería Linda
Vast selection of silverware and jewelry in sterling silver, 14- and 18-carat gold.
✉ **Plaza Borda 4** ☎ **(762) 622 3172**

Pacific Mexico

Acapulco
B & B Gold and Silver Factory
Supplier of many of Acapulco's other jewelry shops. Vast selection.
✉ **Juan Sebastián El Cano 2, by Papagayo Park** ☎ **(744) 483 0441**

Taxco Exporta
Wide selection of silver jewelry from Taxco, including some unique designs. Gold pieces and choice handicrafts too. Bargaining necessary.
✉ **Calle La Quebrada 315 (opposite diving cliff)** ☎ **(744) 482 7165**

Ixtapa-Zihuatanejo
Albertós
This company has been designing and selling unique jewelry in gold, silver and precious stones since 1977.
✉ **Calle Cuauhtémoc No 12 and No 15, Zihuatanejo**
☎ **(755) 554 2161**

The South

Huatulco
Platería Maitl
Original designs in silver jewelry.
✉ **Bugambillas 601C, La Crucecita** ☎ **(958) 587 1223**

Oaxaca
La Bodega del Fraile
Stocks an extensive selection of jewelry at a wide price range. Monte Albán Mixtec replicas, Taxco silver, and more unusual local designs using semi-precious stones.
✉ **Alcalá 501** ☎ **(951) 516 4310**

Jade Artesanias
Oaxacan handicrafts alongside replica jewelry and objects.
✉ **García Virgil 703** ☎ **(951) 516 0519**

Oro de Monte Albán
Fabulous display of gold jewelry reproductions of the Mixtec hoard found at Monte Albán. Fine craftsmanship using lost-wax method. This is one of several outlets.
✉ **Alcalá 403** ☎ **(951) 514 3813**

Sterling Silver
Nearly all sterling silver jewelry and tableware sold throughout Mexico originates in Taxco, so this is where you will find the best prices if you bargain hard. By law, sterling silver must be stamped ".925" which refers to the silver content of the alloy. Always shop around first before buying a particular item, and don't believe that bargains are necessarily found at street stalls.

Children's Attractions

Kids' Outings

The obvious places to take children in Mexico are the beach resorts, where there are endless attractions to keep them happy. Acapulco and Cancún offer the greatest variety, and some hotels give free accommodation to children under 12 if sleeping with their parents. Apart from the places listed, look out for shopping plazas, where video games are usually a standing fixture.

Central Mexico

Mexico City

Feria de Chapultepec

Popular amusement park with over 50 heart-stopping rides, including Mexico's only roller-coaster. Take the "boat trip" down an artificial winding river. Avoid weekends, when lines are long.

✉ **Circuito Bosque de Chapultepec, 2nd section**
☎ **(55) 5230 2112** 🕐 **Tue–Fri 11–6, Sat–Sun 10–9**
🚇 **Constituyentes**

Museo Papalote

A big hit with children and adults as the 250 high-tech exhibits are all interactive. IMAX auditorium shows films on Mexican culture, archaeology and other topics. Located in the second section of Chapultepec park.

✉ **Avenida Constituyentes, Bosque de Chapultepec** ☎ **(55) 5237 1781** 🕐 **Daily 9–1, 2–6**
🚇 **Constituyentes**

El Nuevo Reino Aventura

Southern Mexico City's answer to Disneyland, with over 45 rides, games, a dinosaur show, and other attractions.

✉ **Carretera Picacho – Ajusto 1500** ☎ **(55) 5645 0559**
🕐 **Tue–Thu 10–6, Fri–Sun 10–7**
🚇 **Taxqueña or Universidad, then taxi**

Zoológico de Chapultepec

Spread over 17 hectares, this zoo is home to over 1,600 animals from 270 species. Started by the Aztecs, so claims to be the world's oldest zoo.

✉ **Paseo de la Reforma, Bosque de Chapultepec**
☎ **(55) 5553 6224** 🕐 **Tue–Sun 9–4** 🚇 **Auditorio**

Puebla

Africam

Impressive project that recreates the environment of Africa to preserve and breed endangered species. Lions, tigers, giraffes, rhinos, monkeys, and flamingos can be seen from your own car or park vehicles. Children's zoo and restaurant.

✉ **Km 16.5, Carretera Valsequillo** 🕐 **Daily 10–5**
🚌 **Bus 72 from Boulevard Heroes del 5 de Mayo, Puebla**

Pacific Mexico

Acapulco

Castillo del Rey Leon

New recreation center with pools and small zoo.

✉ **Carretera Pie de la Cuesta, La Barra de Coyuca** ☎ **(744) 481 0192** 🕐 **Daily 9–7**

CICI

Aquariums, dolphins, and water rides keep children more than happy at this well-established park.

✉ **Costera Miguel Alemán** ☎ **(744) 484 8210** 🕐 **Daily 10–6**

Magico Mundo Marino

Combined aquarium and beach club on tiny island off Playa Caleta. Sharks, piranhas, stingrays all visible. Pool with water chute, seal shows.

✉ **Isla La Roqueta** ☎ **(744) 483 1215** 🕐 **Daily 9–6**

Mazatlán

Acuario Mazatlán

Over 50 aquariums with 200 species of fish from all over the world, performing sea lions, botanical gardens, a marine museum, and theater.

✉ **Avenida de los Desportes 111, behind Motel del Sol**
☎ **(669) 981 7815** 🕐 **Daily 9:30–6**

The South

Tuxtla Gutiérrez
Zoológico Miguel Álvarez del Toro
Fabulous zoo where over 200 Central American species roam in large, natural enclosures. Jaguars, quetzals, tapirs, toucans, and more. All in 100 hectares of semi-tropical jungle, on the outskirts of Tuxtla. A pleasant, shady escape from the city.

✉ Off Libramiento Sur Oriente ☎ (961) 614 4701 ⏰ Tue–Sun 9–5

Veracruz
Acuario de Veracruz
Fabulous array of tropical fish in large underwater viewing tank. Sharks and more.

✉ Villa del Mar, Boulevard Ávila Camacho ☎ (228) 932 7984 ⏰ Daily 10–7

Villahermosa
Yumka
Huge jungle and wetlands park with 30-minute boat tour or train through African-type savannah. Good wildlife and children's attractions.

✉ Camino a Yumka, 16km (10 miles) from Villahermosa ☎ (993) 356 0107 ⏰ Daily 9–5

The Yucatán Peninsula

Cancún and Tulum Corridor
Aqua Fun
Marina offering sailing lessons, diving and snorkeling, jetskis, canoes, and waverunners.

✉ Km 16.5, Boulevard Kukulcán, Cancún ☎ (998) 885 2930 ☎ Daily 8–5

Aquaworld
Cancún's largest water-sports centre boasts an underwater "sub see explorer" that glides through coral reefs for a dry close-up of marine life. Also jungle tours, snorkeling and diving lessons.

✉ Km 15, Boulevard Kukulcán, opposite Melia Hotel, Cancún ☎ (998) 885 2288 ⏰ Daily 8AM–10PM

Crocosun
Small zoo 2km (1 mile) north of Puerto Morelos, where visitors can pet or carry animals. The 300 crocodiles are the highlight, besides spider monkeys, white-tailed deer, and Mexican hairless dogs. Includes coffee shop, restaurant, and gift shop.

✉ Km 300, Carretera Cancún-Tulum ☎ (998) 884 4782 ⏰ Daily 8:30–5:30

Wet 'n Wild
Toboggans, water slides, waterchutes and several pools designed for young children. Snorkeling and diving, restaurants, bars, and shops.

✉ Km 25, Boulevard Kukulcán Cancún ☎ (998) 885 1855 ⏰ Daily from 9AM

Xcaret
Vast seaside development with endless attractions, from Mayan temples to underground rivers, aquarium, swimming with dolphins, horseback riding, aviary, butterfly pavilion, orchid farm, and museum.

✉ 8km (5km) south of Playa del Carmen, on Highway 307 ☎ (998) 883 3143/883 3144 ⏰ Daily 8:30AM–10PM

Isla Mujeres
Dolphin Discovery
Swim with dolphins on Isla Mujeres. Well organized but reservations essential. Minimum age 8 years if accompanied by adult, 12 years if not. Day trips from Cancún, ferry leaves from Playa Langosta.

✉ Playa Langosta, Cancún ☎ (998) 883 0777/0779 ⏰ Four swims daily at 9, 11, 1 and 3

Swimming with Dolphins
The Dolphin Discovery Centre in Isla Mujeres has been so successful (more so with adults than children) that it has now expanded its operation to two other Yucatán sites. The largest is in Cozumel, at Laguna Chankanab, where 12 dolphins await play friends, and a second is at Puerto Aventuras (half-way between Playa del Carmen and Tulum), where four dolphins have been trained to dance and perform their astonishing acrobatics (petting permitted).

Nightspots & Shows

Night Culture

Apart from the beach resorts and Mexico City, the rest of the country is not the liveliest place to be in the small hours. However, some recompense may come in the form of local festivals, when brass bands suddenly strike up at 5AM, or in dance and music festivals. All towns have a Casa de Cultura, which will provide information on any upcoming local festivities.

Central Mexico

Mexico City
Ballet Folklórico
Spellbinding panorama of Mexico's diverse traditional dance, music, and costumes from Aztec times to today's fiestas. The best opportunity to witness the country's rich performing arts in one fell swoop. Tickets through hotels or Ticketmaster.
⊠ **Palacio de Bellas Artes**
☎ **(55) 5512 2593/5521 9251**
🕓 **Wed and Sun 8:30PM, Sun 9:30AM** 🚇 **Bellas Artes**

Bar León
Large dance hall with live bands beating out tropical sounds till late. Gets very crowded. Fun, young crowd.
⊠ **Calle Brasil 5, Centro Histórico** ☎ **(55) 5510 3093**
🕓 **Mon–Sat 9PM–3AM**
🚇 **Zócalo**

Bar Mata
Bar on third and top-floor terrace of an historical building. An old favorite for late drinks.
⊠ **Filomena Mata 11, corner 5 de Mayo, Centro Histórico**
☎ **(55) 5518 0237** 🕓 **Tue–Sun 8PM–2AM** 🚇 **Bellas Artes**

The North and Baja California

Los Cabos
El Squid Roe
Without doubt, the craziest restaurant and dance club in Cabo. The place for frenzied dancing all night long.
⊠ **Larazo Cardenas at Boulevard** 🚇 **Marina (624) 143 0655** 🕓 **12PM–3AM or later**

Iguana Bar & Restaurant
Fun, casual place in central San José. Tex-Mex food, dancing waiters, sharp *margaritas*. From 10PM a DJ or live music takes over.
⊠ **Paseo Mijares 8, San José del Cabo** ☎ **(624) 142 0266**
🕓 **11AM–1AM**

Pacific Mexico

Acapulco
Baby'O
Groundbreaking night-spot with dance floor surrounded by tiered spectator seats. Latest sound and light equipment, fast-paced.
⊠ **Costera Miguel Alemán 22, near Hyatt Regency** ☎ **(744) 484 7474** 🕓 **Daily from 10:30PM**

Palladium
The latest night spot in Acapulco, high on hill top. Glass walls give stunning bay views. Techno music dominates.
⊠ **Carretera Escénica Las Brisas** ☎ **(744) 446 5486**

Salon Q
Hot tropical sounds keep the rhythm going in this huge dance spot with live bands. *Salsa, cumbia, merengue* and other Latin beats.
⊠ **Costera Miguel Alemán 23, near La Palapa** ☎ **(744) 481 0114**

Ixtapa-Zihuatanejo
Carlos n' Charlies
Typical resort chain restaurant with lively atmosphere, loud music, and dancing.
⊠ **Paseo del Palmar, next to Hotel Posada Real** ☎ **(755) 553 0085**

La Valentina
More sophisticated than most, but still plenty of atmosphere.
⊠ **Boulevard Ixtapa** ☎ **(755) 553 1190**

Puerto Vallarta

Cactus
Spectacular and popular nightclub in Old Vallarta.
✉ Ignacio L Vallarta 399
☎ (322) 222 6037

Christine's
Classic mainstream disco with wide-ranging music.
✉ Hotel Krystal Vallarta, Zona Hotelera ☎ (322) 224 0202
🕐 Daily 10PM–4AM

Collage
Entertainment center with billiards and backgammon, video games, sushi bar and dance floor.
✉ Calle Proa, at entrance to Marina Vallarta ☎ (322) 221 0505 🕐 Daily 11AM–4AM

Zoo
Central Vallarta's most popular young night spot, easily identified by the giraffe on its roof overlooking the bay. Techno, reggae, house, and disco music. Hard Rock Café is two doors away.
✉ Paseo Díaz Ordáz 630
☎ (322) 222 4945

The South

Huatulco

Magic Circus Disco Club
Domed dance floor attached to Hotel Marlin at western end of Santa Cruz. Mainly international rock. Live bands.
✉ Andador Huatulco 102, Santa Cruz ☎ (958) 587 0017
🕐 Thu–Sat nights

Mágico Trópico
Live tropical and Latino music—*salsa* and more.
✉ Gardenia 311 Altos, opposite Hotel Flamboyant
☎ (958) 587 0702

Poison
Hip nightclub up a dirt road behind the marina. Partly open-air.
✉ Bahía de Santa Cruz
☎ (958) 587 1530

The Yucatán Peninsula

Cancún

La Boom
This is one of Cancún's favorite night spots. Vast disco and adjacent bar, live rock music.
✉ Paseo Kukulcán, near bridge ☎ (998) 883 1152

Cancún Queen
Enjoy a paddle-steamer cruise through the mangroves of Nichupté Lagoon with three-course dinner, live band, dancing, and games.
✉ Aquaworld, Boulevard Kukulcán 15 ☎ (998) 885 5228
🕐 Daily at 6:30PM

Dady'O
Gigantic and legendary disco with tiered seating, blinding laser shows, and mainly techno rhythms.
✉ Km 9.5, Paseo Kukulcán
☎ (998) 883 3333 🕐 Daily from 10PM

Mango Tango
Caribbean exuberance in nightly floor show and sounds.
✉ Boulevard Kukulcán 14.2, opposite Ritz-Carlton Hotel ☎ (998) 885 0303 🕐 Dinner show starts at 8PM daily

Pat O'Brian's
An offspring of the well-known New Orleans bar. Lagoon view, generous drinks, outrageous setting and lots of live piano.
✉ Plaza Flamingo ☎ (998) 883 0418 🕐 Daily 11AM–12:30AM

Roots
Popular restaurant-bar in downtown Cancún with live jazz and blues bands on Thu, Fri, and Sun night. Sat night is flamenco time with dancers and guitarists.
✉ Tulipanes 26 ☎ (998) 884 2437

Dady'O
Cancún's trail-blazing disco has spawned many a follower in other resorts. But it is only here that you will experience 21st-century technology in sound and light systems that some say are the best in the Americas. The nightly three-dimensional laser shows are just a kick-off. If you are in Cancún, don't miss it.

Sports

***Cenote* diving**

This rapidly expanding sport offers an alternative to the depths of the turquoise Caribbean. The limestone shelf of the Yucatán peninsula is riddled with waterways and caverns opening into *cenotes* (sinkholes). Although these are now targeted by diving outfits, remember that *cenote* diving is a dangerous sport and people have lost their lives in the underground labyrinth. Do not attempt this without a guide (► 90).

Central Mexico

Mexico City
Fiesta Charra
Mexico's exciting rodeo. The *charreada* features horsemanship and lassoing skills.
✉ **Rancho del Charro, Avenida Constituyentes 500, Bosque de Chapultepec** ☎ **(55) 5277 8706**
🕐 **Sun noon**
Ⓜ **Constituyentes**

Guadalajara
Expediciones México Verde
Experienced white water rafting agency with expeditions all over Mexico. River-rafting season coincides with rains (Jun–Oct).
✉ **José Maria Vigil 2406, Colonia Italia Providencia, 44610 Guadalajara** ☎ **(33) 3641 5598**

Jalapa
Amigos del Río
White water rafting at all levels in the lush tropical surroundings of the state of Veracruz.
✉ **Calle Chilpancingo 205, Colonia Progreso, 91130 Jalapa** ☎ **(228) 815 8817**

The North and Baja California

Los Cabos
Cabo Aquadeportes
Scuba diving, equipment rental, instructors.
✉ **Hacienda Hotel and Playa Chilena, Cabo San Lucas** ☎ **(624) 143 2062/(800) 733 2226**

Pisces Water Sport Centre
Waterskiing, jetski, windsurfing, banana boats. Snorkeling trips.
✉ **Club Cascadas Beach, Cabo San Lucas** ☎ **(624) 143 1288**

Solmar Fleet
Sport fishing fleet with professional crews and all fishing equipment. For three to ten people.
✉ **Solmar Hotel Desk, Cabo San Lucas** ☎ **(624) 143 0646/(800) 344 3349**

Pacific Mexico

Acapulco
Villa Vera Racquet Club
Acapulco's most famous spot for tennis, to see and be seen.
✉ **Lomas del Mar 35, Fracc Club Deportivo** ☎ **(744) 484 7949**

Ixtapa-Zihuatanejo
Yates del Sol
Speedboat and yacht rental, waterskiing, sunset cruises, snorkeling trips.
✉ **Zihuatanejo** ☎ **(755) 554 2694**

Zihuatanejo Scuba Center
Wide range of diving facilities from beginners to certification courses. Night dives. Marine biologist on call for specialists.
✉ **Calle Cuauhtémoc 3, Zihuatanejo** ☎ **(755) 554 2147**

Puerto Vallarta
Ecotours de Mexico
Kayaking, horseback riding, bird-watching, mountain biking, whale-watching, trekking.
✉ **Ignacio L Vallarta 243** ☎ **(322) 222 6606**

Expediciones Cielo Abierto
Daily adventure trips including kayaking, hiking, and birdwatching. Whale-watching Dec–Mar.
✉ **Guerrero 339, Centro** ☎ **(322) 222 3310; fax: (322) 223 2407**

Pacific Scuba

Diving (PADI certificates) includes night dives, snorkeling at Majahuita beach, Islas Marietas, and Los Arcos. Also offers whale-watching. ✉ **Juárez 722** ☎ **(322) 222 4741**

The South

Huatulco

Eco-Discover Tours

Adventure trips round Huatulco's bays. Specializes in mountain biking and scuba diving but can also arrange horseback riding, kayaking and hiking.

✉ **Plaza Las Conchas L-6, Tangolunda** ☎ **(958) 581 0002**

Jungle Tour

Quad bike (ATV) tours of the jungle around the reserves of Maguey and Organo Bays, with lunch on a beach.

✉ **Lobby of Hotel Royal Maeva, Tangolunda** ☎ **(958) 581 0000**

Oaxaca

Community Museums of Oaxaca

Specialists in all types of eco-tours, including walking, horseback and bicycle trips.

✉ **Constitució** ☎ **(951) 516 2991**

Sociedad Cooperatia Museos Communitarios

Enter the heart of rural communities on accompanied walking tours. Includes crafts demonstrations, lunch and entrance to village museums.

✉ **Tinoco y Palacios 311, Office No 16** ☎ **(951) 516 5786 (and fax)**

Veracruz

Centro de Buceo Curazao

A dive shop that also rents out diving gear and organizes trips. Handles windsurfing and sport fishing as well.

✉ **Boca del Río** ☎ **(228) 822 2033**

Iguana Expediciones

Rafting, kayaking, and scuba diving in the Veracruz area.

✉ **Cotaxtla Sur 16, Colonia Petrolera, Boca del Río** ☎ **(228) 821 1550**

The Yucatán Peninsula

Cancún

Solo Buceo

Scuba diving and snorkeling training and accompanied dives.

✉ **Boulevard Kuklacán – Punta Cancún** ☎ **(998) 884 7070**

Eco-Colors

Adventure tour company. Snorkeling and diving trips, lagoon and jungle trips, tours of Sian Ka'an; 1, 3 or 7 days.

✉ **E-mail: ecoco @cancun.rce.com.mx** ☎ **(998) 884 4950**

Cozumel

Diving Adventures

Scuba diving school, full PADI certificates. Daily boat dives for all levels. Nitrox dives available.

✉ **Calle 5 No 2, San Miguel** ☎ **(987) 872 3009**

Isla Mujeres

Coral Scuba Dive Center

Scuba diving trips, snorkeling.

✉ **Avenida Matamoros 13A** ☎ **(998) 877 0371**

Playa del Carmen

Skydive

Airborne thrills sky diving over the Caribbean with U.S. certified instructor.

✉ **Plaza Marina, Local 32** ☎ **(987) 873 0192**

Tulum

Tak-Be-Ha

Cavern diving, cave and *cenote* snorkeling, jungle treks.

✉ **Highway 307, just south of Xel-Ha** ☎ **(984) 877 8535**
🕐 **Tours daily 9AM, 11AM, 1PM**

The Great Maya Reef

Judged to be the world's second largest coral reef after Australia's Great Barrier Reef, the Palancar Reef extends from Isla Mujeres south to the waters off Belize. This provides endless and fabulous diving and snorkeling opportunities, from Manchones and the Sleeping Sharks' Cave off Isla Mujeres, to sunken galleons off Akumal, and Cozumel's staggering drop-offs and coral-covered tunnels.

What's On When

Fiesta!
Mexico's calendar is not only peppered with national festivals but also with more localized celebrations that may honor a patron saint, an agricultural activity, a seasonal change or re-enact pre-Hispanic rituals. If you can find accommodation during any of the major events, you will witness a colorful, noisy and exuberant side of the Mexican character.

* National public holidays when banks and administrative offices close.

January
1 Jan*: New Year's Day.
6 Jan: Epiphany (Three Kings' Day), celebrated with a special cake.

February
2 Feb: Día de la Candelaria.
5 Feb*: Constitution Day. Shrovetide Carnivals, above all in Veracruz and Mazatlán.

March
21 Mar*: Birthday of Benito Juárez.
21 Mar: Spring Equinox festival in Chichén Itzá.
Easter: Palm Sunday*, Maundy Thursday, Good Friday and Easter Sunday* are the big days. Taxco and the Sierra Tarahumara see the greatest celebrations. Feria de las Flores (flower festival) in Xochimilco on Easter Sunday.

April
San Marcos National Fair in Aguascalientes with *mariachis,* bullfights, rodeos. Late April to early May—varying dates.

May
1 May*: Labor Day.
5 May*: Battle of Puebla (best in Puebla itself). Cancún International Jazz Festival. Varying dates. Acapulco Music Festival. Varying dates.

June
Feast of Corpus Christi in Mexico City. Varying dates.
29 Jun: Tlaquepaque Festival in Guadalajara. *Mariachis,* dances, parades.

July
Third and last Mondays in July: Guelaguetza Festival in Oaxaca. Music and traditional dances by all Oaxaca's indigenous groups.

August
15 Aug: Assumption Day. Streets of Huamantla, Tlaxcala are carpeted with flower-petal designs. Mexico City Cultural Festival. Varying dates.

September
15, 16 Sep*: Independence Day. Military parades and festivities nationwide. President's *grito* on Mexico City's *Zócalo.*
21 Sep: Autumn Equinox Festival at Chichén Itzá.

October
12 Oct*: Día de la Raza (Columbus Day).
Mid- to late-Oct: Cervantino Festival in Guanajuato. Fiestas de Octubre in Guadalajara. Month-long celebrations with dance, *charreadas,* food, arts and crafts exhibits.

November
1 Nov*: Día de Todos los Santos (All Saints' Day).
2 Nov: Día de los Muertos (Day of the Dead). Mexico's fusion of pre-Hispanic and Catholic beliefs comes to the fore. Renowned celebrations at Pátzcuaro, Mixquic, Milpa Alta, Iguala. American-style Halloween is now making inroads on 31 Oct.
20 Nov*: Day of the Revolution.

December
12 Dec: Festival of the much-revered Virgen de Guadalupe. Especially celebrated at the Basílica de Guadalupe, Mexico City.
25 Dec*: Christmas Day.

Practical Matters

Above: *a shady path in San José del Cabo*
Right: *siesta-time, amigo!*

TIME DIFFERENCES

GMT
12 noon

Mexico City
6AM
←

Germany
1PM
→

USA (NY)
7AM
←

Netherlands
1PM
→

Spain
1PM
→

BEFORE YOU GO

WHAT YOU NEED

	Some countries require a passport to remain valid for a minimum period (usually at least six months) beyond the date of entry—contact their consulate or embassy or your travel agent for details.	UK	Germany	USA	Netherlands	Spain
● Required ○ Suggested ▲ Not required						
Passport/National Identity Card		●	●	●	●	●
Visa (Regulations can change—check before your journey)		▲	▲	▲	▲	▲
Tourist Card		●	●	●	●	●
Return Ticket		▲	▲	▲	▲	▲
Health Inoculations		▲	▲	▲	▲	▲
Travel Insurance		●	●	●	●	●
Driving Licence (National)		●	●	●	●	●
Car Insurance Certificate (pay extra daily fee for CDW)		○	○	○	○	○
Car registration document		●	●	●	●	●

WHEN TO GO

Mexico City/Mexico

High season

Low season

19°C	21°C	24°C	26°C	24°C	23°C	23°C	23°C	23°C	21°C	20°C	19°C
JAN	FEB	MAR	APR	MAY	JUN	JUL	AUG	SEP	OCT	NOV	DEC

 Sun   Wet   Sunshine & showers

TOURIST OFFICES

In the U.K.
MexicanTourism Board
Wakefield House
41 Trinity Square
London EC3N 4DJ
☎ 020 7488 9392
Information line:
09065 508917
www.mexicotravel.co.uk

In the U.S.A.
Mexican Tourist Board
375 Park Avenue
Suite 1905
New York
NY 101152
☎ (212) 308 2110
www.visitmexico.com

POLICE, FIRE AND AMBULANCE 080

GREEN ANGELS (Tourist patrol) (55) 5250 8221

For other crisis lines, see local phone book.

WHEN YOU ARE THERE

ARRIVING

Visitors flying into Mexico have the choice between Mexico City and international airports at beach resorts such as Cancún, Los Cabos, Acapulco or Puerto Vallarta. Guadalajara and Puebla are increasingly popular alternatives. All have money-changing facilities, taxis, restaurants, and duty-free shops.

Mexico City Airport Distance to city centre	**Journey Times**	
		20–40 minutes
13 kilometres (8 miles)		N/A
		30–40 minutes

Cancún Airport Distance to city centre	**Journey times**	
		N/A
16 kilometres (10 miles)		30 minutes
		20 minutes

MONEY

The monetary unit of Mexico is the peso ($), divided into 100 centavos. Coins come in10c, 20c, 50c, $1, $2, $5, and $10 denominations. Notes are in $10, $20, $50, $100, $200, and $500. Major credit cards (particularly Visa and MasterCard) are accepted at large hotels, restaurants, travel agents, and stores. Cash machines are widespread, even in small towns. International airports all have money-changing facilities with good rates.

TIME

 Mexico has four time zones. Most of the country runs on Central Standard Time (6 hours behind GMT). The northern states of Nayarit, Sinaloa, Sonora and Baja California Sur are on Mountain Standard Time (7 hours behind GMT). Baja California Norte is on Pacific Standard Time (8 hours behind GMT). Quintana Roo (Cancún) is one hour ahead of Central Standard Time. All regions change their clocks in April and October.

CUSTOMS

 YES

Incoming travelers can bring personal photographic, radio, and sports equipment up to a value of US$300, 3 litres of spirits, 400 cigarettes, perfume, 12 rolls of film or video cassettes, and unlimited foreign currency. A completed customs form must be handed to customs officials and a button pushed: if the red light flashes you are searched, if it is green you pass through.

 NO

Narcotics, weapons, protected wildlife. There are also strict regulations protecting the export of archaeological pieces.

EMBASSIES AND CONSULATES

 UK
(55) 5250 8221

 Germany
(55) 5283 2200

 USA
(55) 5080 2000

 Netherlands
(55) 5258 9921

 Spain
(55) 5280 4508

WHEN YOU ARE THERE

TOURIST OFFICES

Major state tourist offices SECTUR

- Avenida Presidente Masaryk 172, Bosque de Chapultepec, 11587 Mexico DF
  ☎ (55) 5515 2697

- **Baja California Sur**
  Coordinación General de Turismo, Carretera Transpeninsular Km 5.5, Edificio Fidepaz, Apdo Postal 419, 23090 La Paz, Baja California Sur
  ☎ (612) 124 0100

- **Chiapas**
  Secretaría de Desarrollo Turístico
  Blvd Belisario Domínguez 950, 29000 Tuxtla Gutiérrez, Chiapas
  ☎ (961) 612 4535/613 39396

- **Guerrero**
  Acapulco Convention and Visitors Bureau
  Avenue Costera Miguel Alemán 3111
  39850 Acapulco
  ☎ (744) 484 8555

- **Oaxaca**
  Secretaría de Desarrollo Turístico
  Avenida Independencia 607, Centro, 68000 Oaxaca, Oaxaca
  ☎ (951) 515 0717/514 0570

- **Yucatán**
  Departamento de Turismo Calle 59 No 514, Centro, 97000 Mérida, Yucatán
  ☎ (999) 930 3760

NATIONAL HOLIDAYS

J	F	M	A	M	J	J	A	S	O	N	D
1	1	1(1)	(1)	2				1	1	3	1

Jan 1	New Year's Day
Feb 5	Constitution Day
Mar 21	Benito Juárez Day
Mar/Apr	Easter (Maundy Thursday, Good Friday, Easter Sunday)
May 1	Labour Day
May 5	Battle of Puebla
Sep 16	Independence Day (starting eve of 15)
Oct 12	Columbus Day
Nov 1	All Saints' Day
Nov 2	Day of the Dead
Nov 20	Revolution Day
Dec 25	Christmas

OPENING HOURS

○ Shops	● Casa de Cambio
● Offices	○ Museums/Monuments
● Banks	○ Pharmacies

8AM	9AM	10AM	NOON	1PM	2PM	4PM	5PM	7PM

☐ Day   ☐ Mid day
☐ Evening

In hotter areas and coastal resorts, shops close at 1 or 2 for lunch, reopening at 4–5PM and finally closing around 9PM.

Certain banks operate longer hours than above.

Post offices open Monday to Friday 8AM–6PM.

Street markets start at 7AM.

Museums are generally closed on Mondays, and there are regional variations to the opening hours.

**DRIVE ON THE
RIGHT**

**TOILETS
FREE**

or $1

PUBLIC TRANSPORTATION

 Internal Flights Domestic and regional airlines in Mexico are not cheap. Aeromexico and Mexicana have the best schedules and deal with bookings for smaller airlines. Mexicana's Mexipass and Mayapass offer considerable savings if bought in your home country.

 Trains Mexico's neglected train service is really only viable for overnight trains from the U.S. border to Mexico City or Guadalajara, or between the two towns. An exception is the spectacular Chihuahua–Pacífico route (▶ 16). South of the capital, trains are slow, dirty and dangerous.

 Buses The best way of seeing Mexico on a budget. *Primera* (first-class) long-distance bus services are excellent value. Each large town has a *Central Camionera* (bus station) with private lines operating different schedules and routes. For trips over 5–6 hours or during public holidays, buy your ticket a day or so in advance.

 Ferries The Mar de Cortés has three ferry routes: La Paz–Mazatlán; Santa Rosalía–Guaymas; La Paz–Topolobampo. For information ☎ toll-free 01 800 696 9600. The Yucatán peninsula has boats from Playa del Carmen to Cozumel, and Puerto Juárez, Punta Sam (car ferry) or Cancún to Isla Mujeres.

 Urban Transportation Mexico City's metro is excellent and cheap. *Pesero* buses have their destination marked in front, fares are paid to the driver. Elsewhere in Mexico buses and *colectivos* (collective taxis) are easily available, although each city operates different identification systems. Keep small change handy for fares.

CAR RENTAL

 International airports have a large choice of car rental companies. Rates vary considerably. In high season (Dec–Mar) it may be cheaper to pre-book from home. A credit card is required to make a deposit. Check the car before signing the contract.

TAXIS

 Mexico City and nearby towns use meters. Elsewhere, a flat fare is charged or price negotiated in advance. Airport taxis and *colectivos* are expensive. At night in Mexico City, use radio-taxi services (☎ (55) 5519 7690); taxi-muggings are common.

DRIVING

 Speed limit on highways: **110kph**

 Speed limit on country roads: **80kph**

 Speed limit in towns: **60kph**

 Compulsory for front seats.

 Breath testing is not yet developed in Mexico. Due to widespread drinking, as well as hazards such as cattle and speed-breakers, it is not advisable to drive at night.

 Petrol is Nova (leaded) or Magna Sin (unleaded) and is sold by the liter. Pemex (Mexican petrol) stations are plentiful in central Mexico, but fill up at every opportunity when driving in less populated areas. Payment is in cash. Petrol stations close

 For any breakdown anywhere in Mexico, contact the Angeles Verdes (Green Angels). This unique service is free and provides on-the-spot technical assistance or tows. Every state has an Angeles Verdes Hotline so it is advisable to obtain this before setting off.

PERSONAL SAFETY

Sensible precautions should be taken, above all in larger cities. Pickpockets operate in crowded areas such as markets and bus stations, so do not tempt them by exhibiting jewelry, cameras, or thick wallets. Do not leave valuables lying around in your hotel room; use a safety deposit box. Muggings are on the increase in Mexico City (► 121, Taxis) so do not carry anything other than essentials. Elsewhere, avoid taking solitary walks in remote areas or driving after dark. If anything is stolen, report it for insurance purposes.

Police assistance:
☎ **080**
from any call box

TELEPHONES

If possible, bring your own international phone card from home with access number for Mexico. Otherwise, Ladatel (long-distance) booths are easily found and operate with phone cards (30 pesos, 50 pesos, 100 pesos) bought at local stores. Ladatel offices with operators are also widespread. Avoid making long-distance calls from hotels; taxes increase costs.

International Dialling Codes

From Mexico to:	
UK:	00 44
Germany:	00 49
USA & Canada:	00 1
Netherlands:	00 31
Spain:	00 34

POST

Correos (post offices) are in every town center and open Mon–Fri 8–6. Overseas mail is slow but generally reliable, and is a better service than internal post. New red postboxes (*buzón*) are now appearing, although it is safer to post letters at a post office. For anything urgent or of value, use a courier service.

ELECTRICITY

The power supply is 110 volts.
Sockets use two-flat-pin plugs (US style), so Europeans need an adapter and transformer.
Most mid- and upper-range hotels have universal outlets for shavers.

TIPS/GRATUITIES

Yes ✓ No ✗		
Restaurants (service not inc)	✓	10–15%
Cafés/bar	✓	10%
Taxis	✗	
Tour guides	✓	5–10%
Hairdressers	✓	10%
Chambermaids	✓	US$1 per day
Hotel porters	✓	US$1–2
Cloakroom attendants/toilets	✓	$1 (peso)
Petrol-pump attendants	✓	a few pesos

PHOTOGRAPHY

What to photograph: Sierra, cacti, dramatic cliffs, canyons, colonial architecture (do not use flash inside churches), market scenes. Do not photograph the sensitive and troubled indigenous people of Chiapas.

When to photograph: Mexico's clear light at higher altitudes creates strong contrasts. Early morning and late afternoon offer the best light, depending on the quality of your camera.

Where to buy film: Color-print film and processing is widely available. Check expiry dates. Slide film is more difficult to obtain, so stock up in the cities.

HEALTH

Insurance
It is essential to take out a reliable travel insurance policy before leaving home as emergency hospital treatment can be very expensive. For minor ailments pharmacists give good advice, or you can contact a local doctor through your hotel.

Dental Services
Mexican dentists have a very good reputation. If you need emergency treatment, ask at your hotel for a recommendation.

Sun Advice
As in any semi-tropical country, sunburn is an obvious hazard. Do not sunbathe between noon and 3PM and always use a high-factor sun cream. When visiting archaeological sites, wear a hat.

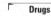

Drugs
Prescription and non-prescription drugs are available from pharmacies (*farmacia*). Bring a basic first-aid kit: mosquito repellent, anti-histamine cream for insect bites, a general antibiotic, pain-relief tablets. Anti-malarial treatment need only be taken if traveling extensively in the rainy season (Jun–Sep) near swamps or lagoons.

Safe Water and Food
Never drink tapwater. *Agua purificada* (purified water) or bottled water is always supplied in hotels and bottled water is widely available. Drink plenty of water to avoid dehydration.

Food
Moctezuma's Revenge (diarrhoea) is a common traveler's complaint in Mexico. Avoid eating salads, uncooked or unpasteurized foods (watch out with ice-creams) and drinks with ice, except in decent hotels and restaurants. The liberal use of lime juice apparently acts as a deterrent against bacteria.

CONCESSIONS

Students/Youths There is little available in the way of reductions for students, as most youth discounts are for Mexican citizens. Children under 12 get reductions on domestic flights and sometimes free beds in their parents' room.

Senior Citizens Again, discounts apply solely to Mexican nationals.

CLOTHING SIZES

Mexico	U.K.	Europe	U.S.A.	
46	36	46	36	Suits
48	38	48	38	Suits
50	40	50	40	Suits
52	42	52	42	Suits
54	44	54	44	Suits
56	46	56	46	Suits
41	7	41	8	Shoes
42	7½	42	8½	Shoes
43	8½	43	9½	Shoes
44	9½	44	10½	Shoes
45	10½	45	11½	Shoes
46	11	46	12	Shoes
37	14½	37	14½	Shirts
38	15	38	15	Shirts
39/40	15½	39/40	15½	Shirts
41	16	41	16	Shirts
42	16½	42	16½	Shirts
43	17	43	17	Shirts
36	8	34	6	Dresses
38	10	36	8	Dresses
40	12	38	10	Dresses
42	14	40	12	Dresses
44	16	42	14	Dresses
46	18	44	16	Dresses
38	4½	38	6	Shoes
38	5	38	6½	Shoes
39	5½	39	7	Shoes
39	6	39	7½	Shoes
40	6½	40	8	Shoes
41	7	41	8½	Shoes

WHEN DEPARTING

- Reconfirm your return flight with the airline 72 hours before departure.
- There is an airport tax on all international flights, payable at check-in in U.S.$ or pesos, unless included in your ticket.
- Check in two hours before departure.

LANGUAGE

Spanish is the language used throughout Mexico, although in large resorts English is also widely spoken. If traveling to smaller places it is essential to know a few basic phrases. Mexican Spanish has slight differences in vocabulary and usage from Castillian Spanish, but otherwise is very similar. Accents change throughout this vast country, and in some areas you will hear local indigenous languages such as Náhuatl, Maya or Zapotec.

Do you have a single/double room?	¿Tiene una habitación sencilla/doble?
For two nights	Para dos noches
With fan/air-conditioning	Con ventilador/aire acondicionado
With double bed/twin beds	Con cama de matrimonio/dos camas
With a balcony/sea view	Con balcon/vista al mar
Is there a swimming-pool?	¿Hay una alberca?
I'd like a towel/soap/toilet-paper/blanket, please	Quisiera una toalla/jabón/papel higiénico/una manta, por favor

How much does it cost?	¿Cuánto cuesta?/¿Cuánta se cobre?
Very expensive/cheap/too much	Muy caro/barato/demasiado
Do you take credit cards?	¿Accepta tarjetas de crédito?
Does that include taxes?	¿Están incluidos los impuestos?
Where is the nearest exchange bureau/bank?	¿Dónde esta la casa de cambio/el banco mas cerca?
I'd like to change traveler's checks	Quiero cambiar unos cheques de viajero
What is the exchange rate?	¿Cuál es el tipo de cambio?

Can I have the menu/bill, please?	El menu/la cuenta, por favor
We'll have two beers please	Dos cervezas por favor
A cup of black coffee (generally weak)/with milk	Un café americano/con leche
Fruit juice	Un jugo de fruta
Fizzy mineral water	Un agua mineral
A bottle of red/white wine	Una botella de vino tinto/blanco

Where is the bus station/railroad-station?	¿Dónde esta el central camionera/la estación del ferrocarril?
How long is the journey?	¿Cuánto tiempo dura el viaje?
straight on/to the left/to the right	Todo derecho/a la izquierda/a la derecha
It's three blocks from here	Está a tres cuadras de aquí
How far is the nearest petrol station?	¿A qué distancia esta la gasolinera mas cerca?

Hello! Good morning	Hola! Buenos días!
Good afternoon	Buenas tardes!
Good night	Buenas noches!
Goodbye/see you	Adiós/hasta luego
Yes/no	Sí/no
Please/thank you	Por favor/gracias
It's a pleasure	De nada
Excuse me, can you help me?	¿Disculpe, me padrí ayudar?
I don't speak Spanish, I'm English (f)	No hablo español, soy inglés (a)
Do you speak English?	¿Habla inglés?
How are you?	¿Cómo está?

INDEX

Acknowledgements
The Automobile Assocation wishes to thank the following photographers, libraries and associations for their assistance in the preparation of this book:

AKG, LONDON 37; HULTON GETTY 11b, 14b; MEXICOLORE 122c (Maricela Gonzalez); MRI Banker's Guide to Foreign Currency 119; LAWSON WOOD 87b.
The remaining photographs are held in the Association's own photo library (AA PHOTO LIBRARY) and were taken by Rick Strange with the exception of the following: 5a, 6a, 6b, 7a, 9a, 10a, 11a, 12a, 13a, 14a, 50, 51, 52, 53, 55, 56a, 56b, 57a, 57b, 58, 59a, 59b, 64a, 68a, 117a which were taken by Robert Holmes and pages 41b, 44, 54, 62b, 70, 84b, 89b, 122a taken by Peter Wilson.

The author would like to thank the following for their assistance: the Mexican Ministry of Tourism in London, Mexico City, Oaxca and Chiapas; Mexicana Airlines, Linda Ambrosie of Tourimex and Jessica Johnson.

Page Layout: Barfoot Design **Revision Management:** Pam Stagg

Dear Essential Traveller

**Your comments, opinions and recommendations are very
important to us. So please help us to improve our travel
guides by taking a few minutes to complete this simple
questionnaire.**

*You do not need a stamp (unless posted outside the UK). If you do not want to cut this page
from your guide, then photocopy it or write your answers on a plain sheet of paper.*

Send to: **The Editor, AA World Travel Guides,
FREEPOST SCE 4598, Basingstoke RG21 4GY.**

Your recommendations...

We always encourage readers' recommendations for restaurants, nightlife
or shopping – if your recommendation is used in the next edition of the
guide, we will send you a **FREE** AA **Essential** Guide of your choice.
Please state below the establishment name, location and your reasons
for recommending it.

_____

_____

_____

_____

Please send me **AA Essential** _____

About this guide...

Which title did you buy?
   AA *Essential* _____
Where did you buy it? _____
When? m̲ m̲ / y̲ y̲

Why did you choose an AA *Essential* Guide? _____

_____

_____

_____

_____

Did this guide meet your expectations?
  Exceeded ☐ Met all ☐ Met most ☐ Fell below ☐
  Please give your reasons _____

_____

_____

_____

continued on next page...

Were there any aspects of this guide that you particularly liked? _____

_____

_____

Is there anything we could have done better? _____

_____

_____

About you...

Name (*Mr/Mrs/Ms*) _____

    Address _____

_____

_____ Postcode _____

    Daytime tel nos _____

Please only give us your mobile phone number if you wish to hear from us about other products and services from the AA and partners by text or mms.

Which age group are you in?
Under 25 ☐   25–34 ☐   35–44 ☐   45–54 ☐   55–64 ☐   65+ ☐

How many trips do you make a year?
Less than one ☐   One ☐   Two ☐   Three or more ☐

Are you an AA member? Yes ☐   No ☐

About your trip...

When did you book? m m / y y   When did you travel? m m / y y
How long did you stay? _____
Was it for business or leisure? _____
Did you buy any other travel guides for your trip?
    If yes, which ones? _____

Thank you for taking the time to complete this questionnaire. Please send it to us as soon as possible, and remember, you do not need a stamp (*unless posted outside the UK*).

Happy Holidays!

Highway, multilane divided road - under construction Autobahn, mehrspurige Straße - in Bau		Auto-estrada, estrada com quatro ou mais faixas - em construção Autopista, carretera de más carriles - en construcción
Trunk road - under construction Fernverkehrsstraße - in Bau		Ruta de longa distância - em construção Ruta de larga distancia - en construcción
Principal highway Hauptstraße		Estrada regional Carretera principal
Secondary road Nebenstraße		Estrada secundária Carretera secundaria
Practicable road, track Fahrweg, Piste		Estrada, pista Camino vecinal, pista
Road numbering Straßennummerierung	MEX 15	Numeração de estrada Numeración de carreteras
Distances in kilometres Entfernungen in Kilometer	130 **259** 129	Quilometragem Distancias en kilómetros
Height in metres - Pass Höhe in Meter - Pass	136 ·	Alture em metros - Desfiladeiro Altura en metros - Puerto de montaña
Railway - Railway ferry Eisenbahn - Eisenbahnfähre		Caminho-de-ferro - Ligação marítima Ferrocarril - Línea marítima
Car ferry - Shipping route Autofähre - Schifffahrtslinie		Batelões para automóveis - Comboios Transportador de automóviles - Ferrocarriles
Major international airport - Airport Wichtiger internationaler Flughafen - Flughafen	✈ ✈	Aeroporto importante internacional - Aeroporto Aeropuerto importante internacional - Aeropuerto
International boundary - Province boundary Internationale Grenze - Provinzgrenze		Fronteira nacional - Limite ou de província Frontera nacional - Frontera provincial
Undefined boundary Unbestimmte Grenze		Incerta fronteira Frontera indeterminada
Time zone limite Zeitzonengrenze	-4h Greenwich Time -3h Greenwich Time	Limite de zona de fuso de tempo Límite del huso horario
National capital Hauptstadt eines souveränen Staates	**MÉXICO**	Capital de país soberano Capital de un estado soberano
Federal capital Hauptstadt eines Bundesstaates	**Durango**	Capital de estado Capital de estado
National park Nationalpark		Parque nacional Parque nacional
Ancient monument Antikes Baudenkmal	∴	Construção da antiguidade Yacimiento arqueológico
Interesting cultural monument Sehenswertes Kulturdenkmal	✳ *Uxmal*	Monumento cultural de interesse Monumento cultural de interés
Interesting natural monument Sehenswertes Naturdenkmal	✳ *Agua Azul* *Cascades*	Monumento natural de interesse Monumento natural de interés
Well Brunnen	‿	Poço Pozo

0		150 km
0		100 miles

Maps © Mairs Geographischer Verlag / Falk Verlag, 73751 Ostfildern

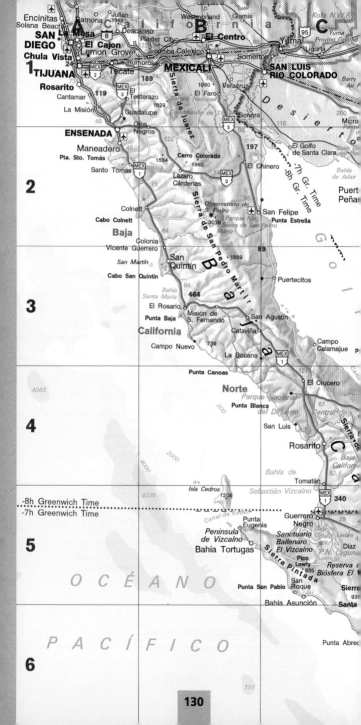

Encinitas
Solana Beach
Julian 1986
Ramona
Westmorland
Glamis
Kofa N.W.R.
SAN DIEGO
La Mesa
El Cajon
Descanso
Plaster City
El Centro
Yuma
Yuma Proving Ground
95
Chula Vista
Lemon Grove
Jacumba Calexico
Somerton
SAN LUIS RIO COLORADO
Ligurta

TIJUANA
Tecate
MEXICALI
Barry Air I

Rosarito
189
1060
Veracruz
MEX 5
Sonora

Cantamar
119
El Testerazo
El Faro
Desierto
200

La Misión
1829
Guadalupe
Micro

ENSENADA
Ojos Negros
El Golfo de Santa Clara
San Do

Maneadero
Cerro Colorado
1980
-7h Gr. Time
Bahía de Adair

Pta. Sto. Tomás
1554
MEX 1
El Chinero
-8h Gr. Time
Puert Peña

Santo Tomás
75
Lázaro Cárdenas
MEX 3
197

Colnett
Observatorio de S. Pedro
3078
San Felipe
Punta Estrella

Cabo Colnett
Parque Nac.
Sierra de San Pedro

Baja
Colonia
1859
89

Vicente Guerrero
San Quintín
Puertecitos

San Martín
Cabo San Quintín
64
464

Bahía Santa María
El Rosario
Misión de S. Fernando
San Agustín

Punta Baja
88
Cataviña

California
Campo Nuevo
739
Campo Calamajue

La Bocana
MEX 1

Punta Canoas
127
El Crucero

Norte
Parque Nacional
Punta Blanca
del Desierto
67
Central de

San Luis
59
Sierra de

Rosarito
Baja Californ

Bahía de
82

Isla Cedros
1205
Tomatán
MEX 1
340

-8h Greenwich Time
-7h Greenwich Time
Canal de Kellet
Guerrero Negro
29

Punta Eugenia
Sebastián Vizcaíno
Sanctuario Ballenaro
Díaz

Península de Vizcaíno
El Vizcaíno
Reserva

Bahía Tortugas
Pico Lowty
935
Biósfera El

OCÉANO
San Roque
Sierra

Punta San Pablo
Bahía Asunción
Santa

PACÍFICO
Punta Abred

130

D **E** **F**

1274

3803

1

G o l f o

3255

d e

2643

M é x i c o 11 **2**

ora

120

ra de Palmas
ga de Alatorre

Quiahniztlan

B a h í a **3**

119

Zempoala
José Cardel
Antigua

d e

VERACRUZ

32 C a m p e c h e

ejas

60 **BOCA DEL RÍO**

oledad Antón Lizardo

Doblado Paso del Toro

71 MEX 180 **87**

ca Tinaja 65 **Alvarado**

Lerdo

Joachín de Tejada Montepío

Tlacotálpan 31

64 Acula Santiago 58 1729

Tierra Blanca Tuxtla 35

Cosamaloapan *Tres Zapotes* Sierra de los Tuxtla Sánchez Tupilco Chiltepec

azca MEX 145 104 Garro 166 Magallanes Carmen Paraíso

res Valles Loma Bonita *Laguna de Catemaco* Agua Comalcalco Jalpa

Juan Villa Azueta **COATZACOALCOS** Dulce Sta. Ana de Mendez

Bautista Cosoleacaque La Venta MEX 180 Comalcalco

Tuxtepec Acayucan 30 54 **MINATITLÁN** 169 **Cárdenas** Cunduacán **VIL**

Isla Sáyula de Morelos Las Choapas T a b a s c o

Valle Playa San Juan Jáltipan(64) Nanchital

onal Vicente **96** Evangelista *Tenochtitlán* Francisco Chontalpa MEX

MEX Xochiapa Rueda Juárez Teapa 195

175 MEX 185 Vasconcelos Pichu- 245

Ixtlán 111 Jesús Carranza calco Vol Chichón

Pde Juárez Choapan MEX 103 **Istmo** Raudales Rayón 5470

(1558) MEX 147 de Malpaso

XACA DE J. 3397 Palomares d e Tecpatán Rayón **5**

ula Yagul Ayutla 33 550 Chicoasén

án Mitla Matías Romero **78** **Tehuantepec** Apitpac Cañón del 44

otlán Totolapan 45 2408 Ocozocoautla Sumidero Soyaló

PAN Cd. Cintalapa MEX **TUXTLA** Ch.

María 47 **209** Magd. Juárez Ixtepec La Ventosa de Figueroa 130 **GUTIÉRREZ** de C

juitlán Yautepec Tequisistlán de Zaragoza U. Hidalgo **91** S. Pedro **58** Las Cruces (530)

iahuatlán 70 1050 40 *La* S.Dionisio Tapanatepec 48 3202 Villa

atlán 3139 Sto. Domingo *Inferior* del Mar Sta. MEX 195 Flores

Co. León Sta. Ma. Tehuantepec *Superior* S. Fco. **42** Isabel Sierra Buenavista

San Pedro Ecatepec Ixhuatán Pto. Arriaga Madre

el Alto MEX **Salina Cruz** Palomas **Tonalá 6**

MEX **196** San Pedro MEX 200 Mar Muerto Paredón **202**

175 María Huamelula G o l f o d e Pto. Arista MEX

Sta Sta. Cruz Huatulco T e h u a n t e p e c 200 de Ch

Huatulco **141** 53 Pijijiapan

A

1
G o l f o
d e
2643
11

B

Arrecifes
🪸 *Triángulos*

C

Arrecife
Mada
Arrecife Sisal

Sisa
Parque Natural
Ría Celestún
Hunuc
8 Celestún
Punta Nimún
Kino

Maxcan

La Costa

Becal
Calkini

2
M é x i c o
B a h í a
d e

Isla Cayos Arcas

Hecelchakán
42
Tenabó
Be
Che

CAMPECHE
Lerma
Punta Morro
64
Hool
74
Pich
E

C a m p e c h e

Champotón
16

Pustunich
Pustunich
Pixoyal
250

3
Península *147*
El Palmar
Isla del
Carmen
Nuevo
Campechito
**CIUDAD
DEL CARMEN**
Isla 45
de Aguada
Dieciocho
de Marzo
84
Chicbul
Escárcega

15

Pta. Frontera
Frontera
192
Atasta
Zacatal
MEX
180
Laguna
de Términos
Silvituc
El Tigre

Tupilco
Chiltepec
Comalcalco
Sta. Ana
Paraiso
Jalpa
de Mendez
169
MEX
180
Cárdenas
Cunduacán
VILLAHERMOSA
MEX
186
Ciudad
Pemex
Emiliano
Zapata
Chablé
Catazaja
Tulipán

El Vapor
Palizada
Jonuta

Candelaria
El Triunfo
Balancán
de Domínguez
MEX
186

c a m p e c
Caribe
Ca

Nueva Coahuila
El Mira
del Tigre Dos Lagunas

4
Chontalpa
Juárez
Pichu-
calco
Raudales
de Malpaso
Teapán
Apitpac
550
Rayón
245
Vol.
Chichón
2470
Jalapa
Teapa
Palenque
Palenque
Agua Azul
Cascadas Waterfall
Yajalón
Tzinteel
Simojovel
de Allende
Chicoasén
Gregorio
Méndez
La Palma
Piedras Negras
El Cayo
La Mar
Tenosique
de Pino Suárez
421
Carmelita
La Florida
Sierra del Lacandón
Yaxchilán
San Be

5
Soyaló
Chamula
**TUXTLA
GUTIÉRREZ**
(530)
Ch.
de Corzo
Acala
Zinacantán
San Cristóbal
de las Casas
137 Amatenango
del Valle
2224
Chamula
Las
Rosas
Venustiano
Carranza
Presa
La
Concordia
La Trinitaria
Comitán
de Domínguez
Las
Margaritas
Iziscao
Laguna
de Montebello
S.Mateo Ixtatán
Barillas
Lacanjá
Bonampak
El Planchón
Altar de
Sacrificios
El
Pabellón
Sayaxché
Aguatec
San Gregorio
Lagartero
Pedro
Vega

Larrainzar Cancuc
Tenejapa Tonina
Altamirano
Ocosingo
Temo
Lacanja

3202
Villa
Flores
Tonalá
Pto. Arista
202
130
cozocoautla
48
Sierra Madre de Chiapas
Buenavista
Chicomuselo
Frontera
Comalapa
Co. Tres
Cruces
2949
3050
Motozintla
de Mendoza
San
La
Mesilla
CA1
Sierra de los Cuchumatanes
3764
Soloma
Cobán
Sta.Cruz
Chisec

6
Pijijiapan
Mapastepec
Acapetagua
Huixtla
Tapachula
Mazatán
Pto. Madero
La Tembladoras
200
Unión
Juárez
El
Carmen
Vol. Tacana 221
4093
V.Tajumulco
4220
142
S.Pedro
Sacatepéquez
Huehuetenango
Zaculeu
Sta.Lucía
La Reforma
Utatlán
Totonicapán
QUEZALTENANGO
Solola
S.Atitlan
Sacapulas
Sta.Cruz
del Quiché
Cubulco Salamá
5
Joyabaj
129
Chimal-
tenango
Mixco
GUATE
CA9
(1500)
Pajapita
Sta.Cruz
Chinkultic

Parque Natural San Felipe
Pto. Chicxulub
Dzilam de Bravo
Telchac
MÉRIDA
Motul
Izamal
Hoctún
Conkal
Izamna
Kantunil
Piste
Tixkokob
Sotuta
Tekit
Yaxcaba
Oxkutzcab
Kabah
Tekax de Á. C.
Labná
Ichmul
Peto
Tzucacab
X-Pichil
Polyuc
Becanchén
Iturbide
Dzibalchén
Xpujil
pujil
Tomás Garrido
villahermosa
Balakbal
Río Azul
axactún
Tikal
Naranjo
Nakum
Xunantunich
Caracol
Ixcún
Dolores
Luis
Modesto Méndez
El Estor
Minas
Zacapa
Chiquimula

Pta. Holchit
San Felipe
Río Lagartos
Panabá
52
Tizimín
Espita
Temax
Xlacah
Cenotillo
Dzitás
Chichén Itzá
Valladolid
Chemax
Cobá
Tekom
Ekbalám
El Ideal
Tihosuco
Tepich
Chumpón
Sta. Rosa
Laguna Chichancanab
Vigia Chico
Felipe Carrillo Puerto
Petcacab
Valle Hermoso
Cafetal
Ursulo Galván
Bacalar
CHETUMAL
Corozal
Sta. Rita
Kohunlich
Pucté
Orange Walk
El Posito
Altún Ha
Lamanaí
BELIZE
Belize City
Hattieville
Belmopan
Buena Vista
San Ignacio
Cd. Melchor de Mencos
Victoria Peak
Nim Li Punit
San Antonio
Punta Gorda
Tres Puntas
Puerto Barrios
Castillo de San Felipe
Lago de Izabal
Frances
Quiriguá
Nva. Arcadia
Sta. Bárbara
Sta. Rosa de Copán
Copán Ruinas

Cabo Catoche
Isla Holbox
I. Contoy
El Cuyo
Chiquilá
I. Mujeres
Pto. Juárez
Cancún
Cancún
Buenaventura
Vicente Guerrero
Playa del Carmen
Xcaret
Pta. Molas del Norte
Puerto Aventuras
Xcacel
Akumal
Cozumel
Isla de Cozumel
Cedral
Tulum
Tulum
Pta. Celarain
Chamax
Pta. Allen
Bahía de la Ascensión
Sian Ka'an Reserva de la Biósfera
Chacmool
del Espíritu Santo
Pta. Herrero
Pto. Madero
Majahual
Cayo Norte
Banco Chinchorro
Cayo Centro
Cayo Lobos

Península
de Yucatán

Mar
Caribe

Hicks Cays
Turneffe Islands
Northern Cay
Drowned Cays
Lighthouse Reef
Long Cay
Southern Long Cays
Columbus Cay
Dangriga
Tobacco Range
Belize Barrier Reef
Reserve System
Riversdale
Glovers Reef
Mango Creek
Golfo de Honduras
Ranguana Cay
Sapodilla Cays
Isla de Guanaja (Hon.)
P.N.Marino Barbareta
Guanaja
Isla de Roatán (Hon.)
Roatán
Islas de la Bahía (Hon.)
Isla de Utila
Utila
Puerto Castilla
Cabo de Honduras
Puerto Cortés
Tela
La Ceiba
Trujillo
Omoao
Jilamo
Pico Bonito
Jutiapa
Savá
SAN PEDRO SULA
La Lima
EL PROGRESO
Masica
Cordillera
Nombre de Dios
San José
Olanchito
Canoa
El Negrito
Pueblo Viejo
M. de Yoro
La Unión
S. Francisco de la Paz
Marale
Salamá
Catacami
San Francisco de Juticalpa
Orica
La Libertad

Quintana Roo

HONDURAS

143

Sight Locator Index

This index relates to the atlas section on pages 130–143. We have given map references to the main sights of interest in the book. Some sights in the index may not be plotted on the atlas. Note: ibc – inside back cover

For the main index see pages 125–126